THE *Ascent* OF
Mount Carmel

Saint John of the Cross

REFLECTIONS

ICS Publications
2131 Lincoln Road NE
Washington, DC 20002-1199
800-832-8489
www.icspublications.org

All Scripture passages are taken from the *New Revised Standard Version: Catholic Edition, Anglicized Text*, ©1999, 1995, 1989, Division of Christian Education of the National Council of Churches of Christ in the United States of America. Used with permission.

The Screwtape Letters by C.S. Lewis © C.S. Lewis Pte. Ltd., 1942, extract reprinted by permission.

Back cover author photo © Randy Hill, 2013, published with permission; R.B. Hill Photography, LLC; www.rbhillphoto.com

Book and cover design and pagination by Rose Design

Produced and printed in the United States of America

Library of Congress Cataloging-in-Publication Data

Foley, Marc, 1949-
  The ascent of Mount Carmel : reflections / Marc Foley. -- First edition
    pages cm
  Includes bibliographical references and index.
  ISBN 978-1-939272-11-9 (alk. paper)
  1. John of the Cross, Saint, 1542-1591. Subida del Monte
Carmelo. 2. Mysticism--Catholic Church. I. Title.
    BV5082.3.J643F65 2013
    248.2'2--dc23
                                    2013009722

ISBN 978-1-939272-11-9

THE Ascent OF Mount Carmel

Saint John of the Cross

REFLECTIONS

MARC FOLEY, O.C.D.

ICS Publications
Institute of Carmelite Studies
Washington, D.C.

OTHER BOOKS BY MARC FOLEY, O.C.D.

St. Teresa of Avila – The Book of Her Foundations: A Study Guide
ICS Publications, 2011

*The Context of Holiness: Psychological and Spiritual Reflections
on the Life of St. Thérèse of Lisieux*
ICS Publications, 2008

The Path to Merciful Love: 99 Sayings by Thérèse of Lisieux
New City Press, 2007

Peace of Heart: Reflections on Choices in Daily Life
New City Press, 2007

A Season of Rebirth: Daily Meditations for Lent
New City Press, 2007

The Story of a Soul by St. Thérèse of Lisieux: A Study Edition
ICS Publications, 2005

The Ascent to Joy: St. John of the Cross
New City Press, 2002

*The Love That Keeps Us Sane:
Living the Way of St. Thérèse of Lisieux*
Paulist Press, 2000

*In gratitude to my dear friend
Sandra Gettings for her editorial assistance*

CONTENTS

Preface

❧

Pope John Paul II was convinced that the church's "great challenge" in this new millennium is to make the church the "home and school of communion."[1] A more contemplative church will surely bring about a deeper communion within the church and make the church a better partner in ecumenical and interreligious dialogue so that the prayer of Jesus may be achieved: "That they may be one, as we are one, I in them and you in me, that they may become completely one" (Jn 17:22–23). A major resource for making the church more contemplative is the Carmelite tradition. As St. Teresa of Jesus wrote, "All of us who wear this holy habit of Carmel are called to prayer and contemplation."[2] John of the Cross, Teresa's collaborator in the reform of Carmel, with his incomparable poems and commentaries remains in this millennium a singular guide for all who seek to live and pray more contemplatively.

The writings of Teresa de Jesús were read avidly during her lifetime and ever since. That has not been the same scenario for Juan de la Cruz. Some of his poems are acknowledged as some of the best ever composed in Spanish while his commentaries and other writings have made him a mystic's mystic. Yet, over the centuries there were complicated reasons why John of the Cross has been neglected. From the late seventeenth century onwards an anti-mystical stance asserted itself in the Catholic tradition. That attitude survived until the middle of the twentieth century when Christians began to realize the toll that this anti-mystical strain had taken on the vitality of Christian spirituality. Thomas Merton's writings signaled a new welcoming of contemplative wisdom, and a very new moment came with the Second Vatican Council's "Universal Call to Holiness," a holiness that contemplative prayer enhances.

Since Vatican II many contemplative voices have been heard, not the least of which is the contemplative wisdom of the three Carmelite doctors of the church, Teresa, John, and Thérèse. Although there has been a growing interest in the contemplative wisdom of John of the Cross, there linger suspicions that John of the Cross is too demanding for the ordinary Christian. Modern scholarship has amply shown that, indeed, John was anything but harsh; in fact, he was an attentive, gentle, and compassionate friar. More importantly the wisdom in John's writings about human nature, its weaknesses and foibles, and its call to union with God is spiritual fare much needed for the pilgrims on the path to holiness. John of the Cross's gifted insights into how humans become open to God's lavish love are unique and insightful—in fact, precious beyond saying for any community whose members seek to become more contemplative.

One of the reasons that some readers give up on John of the Cross is that they encounter him for the first time in *The Ascent of Mount Carmel*. Besides not yet catching his full stride in how to compose a commentary, John deals in *The Ascent* with one of the most intractable challenges facing the human person: the freedom to be loved as well as the freedom to love. That journey to freedom is no "cheap grace." The demands of that journey to freedom are illustrated throughout *The Ascent of Mount Carmel* where John despite these demands wisely guides his readers to a "sweet and delightful freedom."[3]

In courses that I have taught on John of the Cross I have regularly recommended that *The Ascent* be studied only after John's poetry and after one has read a text like *The Living Flame of Love.* But now I shall also recommend that students consult Father Marc Foley's *The Ascent of Mount Carmel: Reflections.* For a long time I have heard from students about the depth and the inspiration of Father Marc's courses on Carmelite classics. Now in these reflections it is clear to me why Father Marc so inspires his students.

With this book my students and I now have what you will have: a very able guide to *The Ascent of Mount Carmel.* Father Marc is a seasoned reader of John of the Cross who shares with his readers the wisdom he has gained through the years from *The Ascent.* John of the Cross lived and wrote in a very different religious culture that had its own ways of exploring the spiritual issues of the day and that used a vocabulary that now needs to be translated through illustrations that fit the experience of twenty-first-century spiritual pilgrims. Father Marc does this translation skillfully, and what he does in this regard will make new readers gain confidence as they read John's text. John admits that his style in *The Ascent* is "awkward" and that his doctrine "appears somewhat obscure."[4] Yet, Father Marc addresses these issues deftly and thoroughly.

A special gift that Father Marc brings to his role as an interpreter of the teachings of John of the Cross is the breadth and depth of his reading in literature. With ease he consults religious figures like Augustine, John Cassian, Thomas Aquinas, Dante, and Francis de Sales, as well as so-called secular authors like Shakespeare, William Blake, Charles Dickens, Fyodor Dostoyevsky, and C. S. Lewis. Great literary authors explore humanity's suffering and tragedies but also humanity's struggles to flourish amid these obstacles. John of the Cross addresses these very same humans.

John of the Cross is one of the spiritual authors in the West who is explicit in his writings about the theme of deification in the spiritual life, that is, the process whereby one becomes God-like. What we sometimes forget is that deification is, in fact, a way in which God sees to it that we become fully human. Father Marc's extensive reading in both religious and humane literature is thus able to bring together creatively what too often is separated into the religious and the so-called profane. As T. S. Eliot has expressed it, "The hint half guessed, the gift half understood, is Incarnation," the great saving union of the divine and the human.[5] John of the Cross was an extraordinary poet, well versed in the poetry of his time, as well as adept in philosophy and theology. His contemplative wisdom is stunning, too valuable to be left on a bookshelf. Father Marc Foley's splendid grasp of human nature enhanced by his training in psychology as well as his keen and extensive reading of literature make him a very able guide to John of the Cross's contemplative wisdom.

I always advise readers of John of the Cross to keep the Bible at one elbow and John's poetry at the other. Now I shall recommend that they read Father Marc's reflections on *The Ascent of Mount Carmel* ahead of time and that they keep those reflections close by as they read John of the Cross's *Ascent*.

The barriers of time, language, and culture can impede our access to significant classics like John of the Cross's *Ascent of Mount Carmel*, but Father Marc Foley has made access to *The Ascent* much less formidable than it has been for those now called by Vatican II to that genuine holiness that the Carmelite tradition portrays as culminating in transformation in God through love.

Keith J. Egan, T. O. Carm.

Translation and Abbreviations

All quotations are taken from *The Collected Works of St. John of the Cross*, translated by Kieran Kavanaugh, O.C.D., and Otilio Rodriguez, O.C.D. (Washington, DC: ICS Publications, 1991). The abbreviations for John's works are as follows:

A   *The Ascent of Mount Carmel*
C   *The Spiritual Canticle*
Co   *The Counsels*
F   *The Living Flame of Love*
Lt   *Letters*
N   *The Dark Night of the Soul*
Pre *The Precautions*
SLL *The Sayings of Light and Love*

Regarding references to both *The Ascent* and *The Dark Night*, the first number indicates the book, the second number refers to the chapter, and the third number refers to the paragraph. For example, A.2.3.4 refers to book two, chapter 3, paragraph 4 of *The Ascent*. In like manner, for *The Spiritual Canticle* and *The Living Flame of Love*, the first number refers to the stanza and the second number to the paragraph. Thus, C.3.4 is a reference to stanza 3, paragraph 4 of *The Spiritual Canticle*.

All quotations of St. Teresa of Avila are taken from the Kieran Kavanaugh, O.C.D., and Otilio Rodriguez, O.C.D., translation of *The Collected Works of St. Teresa of Avila*, 3 vols. (Washington, D.C.: ICS Publications, 1976–1985, 1987, 2012). The abbreviations for St. Teresa's works are as follows:

L   *The Book of Her Life*
F   *The Book of Her Foundations*
W   *The Way of Perfection*
SS *Meditations on the Song of Songs*
IC *The Interior Castle*

For the first four works, the first number refers to the chapter, and the second number refers to the paragraph. Thus, L.3.5 refers to *The Book of Her Life*, chapter 3, paragraph 5. Regarding *The Interior Castle*, the first number refers to the dwelling place; the second number refers to the chapter, and the third number refers to the paragraph. Thus, IC.3.4.2 refers to the third dwelling place, chapter 4, paragraph 2.

All quotations of St. Thérèse of Lisieux are taken from the John Clarke, O.C.D., translations of her works by ICS Publications. The abbreviations for St. Thérèse's works are as follows:

S   *Story of a Soul*
L   [The Collected Letters], *St. Thérèse of Lisieux, General Correspondence*, vols. 1, 2.

The number following the letter refers to the page of the ICS edition of the work cited. Thus, S.13 refers to page 13 of *Story of a Soul,* third edition, 1996.

All Scripture passages are taken from the *New Revised Standard Version: Catholic Edition, Anglicized Text,* ©1999, 1995, 1989, Division of Christian Education of the National Council of Churches of Christ in the United States of America. Used with permission. All Scripture passages are taken from the *New Revised Standard Version: Catholic Edition, Anglicized Text,* ©1999, 1995, 1989, Division of Christian Education of the National Council of Churches of Christ in the United States of America. Used with permission.

A Hard Book to Read

Both the subject matter and style of the writings of St. John of the Cross make his works difficult to understand. John's subject matter cannot be fully comprehended because he writes of the interrelationship between God's grace and the human soul, both of which are mysteries. Even John admits that he cannot fully explain the spiritual graces that he has received. "Who can describe in writing the understanding God gives to loving souls in whom He dwells? And who can express the desires He gives them? Certainly, no one can! *Not even they who receive these communications*" (C. Prol.; italics added). However, this does not mean that nothing can be communicated. For John also says that "something of their experience overflow[s] in figures, comparisons and similitudes" (C. Prol.).

In *The Ascent of Mount Carmel*, John uses many similitudes and comparisons in expounding his thought. While they are helpful, they sometimes prove to be frustrating because they lack the clarity that only real-life examples can provide.

Another frustration that many people encounter in reading John is his use of Scholastic terminology. John presupposes that his audience has an acquaintance with the basic concepts of Scholastic philosophy; however, most of us do not.

Finally, John does not make a good first impression. The prose style in *The Ascent* is often stark, repetitious, and at times, unintelligible. This book attempts to make *The Ascent* both comprehensible and relevant to daily life.

COMING TO TERMS

Reading the opening chapters of *The Ascent of Mount Carmel* is like walking into a room where a conversation is in progress. You hear words that are unfamiliar to you, such as "dark night," "beginner," "proficient," and "perfect." But since you don't want to interrupt the lively exchange, you follow the conversation as best you can, hoping that something will be said that will clarify your confusion. However, this doesn't happen, and you leave the room bewildered. This analogy is apt, for in the prologue of *The Ascent*, John uses terms that he does not define. Therefore, as we begin considering *The Ascent*, let us examine John's terminology.

THE DARK NIGHT

The dark night can never be completely understood because it is the mystery of God's presence in our lives. As John writes, "The dark night is an inflow of God into the soul . . . [who] teaches the soul secretly and instructs it in the perfection of love" (N.2.5.1). It is God's presence that invites us to choose to do his will.

Let us consider one example:

As you greet a coworker, you sense from his demeanor that something is bothering him. Instinctively, you feel that

God is prompting you to ask him, "Is everything okay? You seem troubled." However, you hesitate to ask because you do not want to become involved in a time-consuming conversation. We all know the inner struggle at such moments as we experience the conflict between God's invitation to love and our resistance.

This conflict is at the heart of what John means by the dark night. As God's presence comes into our lives and invites us to let go of all that is contrary to God's will for us, we resist. We know that our ultimate happiness depends upon surrendering to God's will; nevertheless, we resist and tenaciously cling to our own.

However, the dark night is complex. It encompasses all modes of God's presence in the soul and the soul's vast range of responses. This complexity is mirrored in John's subdivisions of the dark night: the active night of sense, the passive night of sense, the active night of the spirit, and the passive night of the spirit. To understand these subdivisions, let us clarify John's terms *sense/spirit* and *active/passive*.

SENSE

For John, the soul refers to the *whole* of the human person. Its two major divisions are sense and spirit. Sense includes the five bodily senses and the interior senses of the imagination, phantasy, and sense memory.

(Readers may have noted the spelling of *phantasy* here, which will be used throughout this book. There are two reasons for which *phantasy* seemed preferable to the more common *fantasy*. The first is to clearly distinguish John's use of the word from the contemporary, popular meaning of "fantasy" as something which has no basis in reality, or is imaginary—as in Disney's "Fantasyland" or the old TV program, "Fantasy Island." John's use of *fantasia* in Spanish does not mean imaginary or make-believe, but rather refers to a type of interior "storage place" or archive for the forms or apprehensions of the imagination and memory. The second reason for using this spelling is to match the usage and spelling of this term in the Kavanaugh/Rodriguez text of John's collected works, which is the source for this book's citations.)

All of these components—the five bodily senses and the interior senses of the imagination, phantasy, and sense memory—are interrelated and work together. The five bodily senses receive impressions from the external world, the sense memory stores them, and the imagination and phantasy construct them. For example, most of us have seen bananas and the color pink. If we want to see a pink banana, all we need to do is close our eyes. Our imagination will do the rest. It will place an order to our sense memory for "pink" and "banana" and will construct a "pink banana" for our amusement.

As we read either *The Ascent* or *The Dark Night*, being cognizant that the term *sense* includes the mental powers of imagination and phantasy will help us to understand some very obscure passages. For example, when John writes about the transition from discursive meditation (a form of prayer that employs the imagination and phantasy) to contemplative prayer, he frequently refers to the imagination and phantasy with phrases such as "interior sense faculties" or "the senses." For example, John writes, "If souls are to advance, they will ever enter further into the purgation and leave further behind their work of the senses" (N.1.9.9). Thus, John is saying that when God is drawing a soul into contemplative prayer, it must cease to force itself to meditate by constructing images by means of the imagination and phantasy, or "the senses."

SPIRIT

The spirit, or the "higher part" of the soul, consists primarily of the faculties of the intellect, memory, and will. They are not objects but rather our capacities to know, to desire, and to love. Because we are made in the image and likeness of God, we seek to know and to love that which is infinite, for nothing less will satisfy the human heart. "The soul's faculties . . . are as deep as the boundless goods of which they are capable since anything less than the infinite fails to fill them" (F.3.18). Included in the term *spirit* is "the substance of the soul," which refers to the deepest and most inward part of the human person. It is the point of encounter between the human and the divine where God can communicate to the soul directly, without the mediation of the exterior senses.

Scholastic philosophy, following Aristotle, teaches that all knowledge originates with sense experience (A.1.3.3). However, by positing the substance of the soul, John is saying, "Aristotle is right but with *one* exception. God can bypass the senses and touch us from the 'inside,' so to speak." To use an image, the five senses can be compared to five doors that lead into a castle, and the substance of the soul is like a trap door, located in the deepest recesses of the castle, through which God can enter.

RELATIONSHIP BETWEEN SENSE AND SPIRIT

While sense and spirit are distinct entities, they are not separate from one another. In short, we are a psychosomatic unity, a creature in which our physical, psychological, and spiritual processes work together. To use John's words, sense and spirit form a "whole harmonious composite" (N.2.11.4).

The unity of sense and spirit contains a twofold truth. First, we are purified on both levels of our being (sense and spirit) simultaneously. Second, the purification of sense is not complete until the spirit is transformed.

Sometimes John gives the impression that the purification of sense and spirit are two separate processes and that it is only after the night of sense is completed that the night of the spirit begins. While there is some truth in the linearity of the two nights, they often overlap and take place simultaneously.

PASSIVE AND ACTIVE

Just as sense and spirit are two interrelated parts of our soul, so passivity and activity are two inseparable dimensions of our purification and transformation. John uses the word passive in two ways. First, it refers to our relationship to God's grace, which is always receptive or passive. We are the recipients of God's continuous presence that guides, enlightens, strengthens, and consoles us. The active dimension of purification is our response to God's presence. In short, we must act upon the grace that is given. Let us take a common example of the interrelationship between the passive (God's invitation) and active (our response) dimensions of the dark night.

John writes that "the dark night is an inflow of God into the soul . . . which instructs us in the perfection of love without [the soul] doing anything or understanding how it happens" (N.2.5.1). For example, in the midst of a conversation with a coworker, you are tempted to respond with a cruel or catty remark. The remark is on the tip of your tongue when a feeling deep inside you says, "Don't!" This "feeling" is God instructing you in love, without you doing anything or understanding how it happens. It just seems to happen. This is an experience of God inviting you to fast from evil. The choice to bridle your tongue is your active response.

John also uses the word passive to refer to a specific form of purification. The Spanish verb *padecer*, translated as passive, means to endure, to undergo, or to suffer. In passive purification, the soul must endure various sufferings. In particular, John focuses on two sufferings: first, the feeling that one has been abandoned by God (when, in fact, God is deeply present to the soul); and second, the feeling of being overwhelmed by one's sense of sinfulness as God's searing light invades the soul.[1]

FOURFOLD NIGHT

There are four different combinations of the terms *sense*, *spirit*, *active*, and *passive* that result in four subdivisions of the one dark night: the active night of sense, the passive night of sense, the active night of the spirit, and the passive night of the spirit. Let us briefly examine the nature of each subdivision.

ACTIVE NIGHT OF SENSE

John calls the active night of sense "the point of departure" ("*termino donde el alma sale*"; A.1.2.1). This metaphor for the first stage of the dark night contains a fundamental truth about life, namely, that every beginning is linked to an ending. Every choice is an end point from which we depart. It is a *termino* (an end) from where we *sale* (go forth). To embark means to depart; to go ahead is to leave behind. We can only make a new beginning in life when we give up an old way of living. This is an inexorable truth from which there is no escape. Not to indulge one's appetites is to deprive them. As T. S. Eliot so aptly put it, "To make an end is to make a beginning. The end is where we start from."[2]

The active night of sense deals with the obvious. Its focus is on behavioral change: correcting obvious faults, choosing to mortify our self-centered ego, and exercising restraint regarding sensory pleasures. Though the pleasures may not be sinful in themselves, our inordinate indulgence in them makes us lethargic in responding to God's will. The night of sense consists of "bridling" our appetites (N.2.3.1), reining in our desires, and "pruning" the behavioral branches of our lives (N.2.2.1). The purpose of the active night of sense is not to repress desire but to reorient it. It is the soul's first attempt to change its life-organizing principle from the pursuit of pleasure and the avoidance of pain to living a life of virtue by doing God's will.

But what makes it possible for a soul to give up its accustomed pleasures? What provides it with the strength to climb out of its entrenched habits? John says that it is an inflow of God into the soul in the form of consolation. Consolation is pleasure that weans the soul away from the things of this world to the things of God.

A love of pleasure and attachment to it usually fires the will toward enjoying things that give pleasure. A more intense enkindling of another, better love (love of the soul's Bridegroom) is necessary for vanquishing the appetites and denying this pleasure. By finding satisfaction and strength in this love, the soul will have the courage and constancy to readily deny all other appetites (A.1.14.2). In short, God is luring the soul away from the pleasures of earth by means of the pleasures of heaven.

But isn't there a danger that the soul will become addicted to a new form of pleasure? Yes! In fact, some do. "Some others let themselves be encumbered by the very consolations and favors God bestows on them for the sake of their advancing, and they advance not at all" (A. Prol. 7). So why does God take this chance?

God is wise. God knows that the modus operandi of these souls is to seek satisfaction; they are ruled by the pleasure principle. Therefore, since at this early stage of the spiritual journey these souls are too weak to act against the main motivating force of their lives, God uses this weakness to their own advantage. By making prayer and the exercise of virtue consoling, God weans these souls away from sinful and self-destructive behaviors. It is as if God is saying, "I know that these souls are praying and practicing virtue for the same reason they used to pursue the goods of the world—it feels good. And down the road I will have to purify their motive. But first, I need to get them headed in the right direction."

John calls the type of prayer practiced at this stage discursive meditation. It is a step-by-step form of prayer that employs the senses and the imagination. For example, after individuals read a passage from the Gospels (e.g., Jesus in the Garden of Gethsemane), they will close their eyes and try to imagine the scene (composition of place) and then reflect upon the scene by asking various questions (e.g., Who is this person? What is happening here? etc.). Such reflection will elicit sentiments (e.g., sorrow) that will find expression in speech, by which the individuals will speak directly to Jesus (vocal prayer). For souls at this initial stage, meditation is consoling, and the practice of virtue is effortless. But all this changes when God withdraws his consoling presence.

ACTIVE NIGHT OF THE SPIRIT AND PASSIVE NIGHT OF SENSE

When the sweet breast of consolation is withheld, God does not withdraw. Rather, the mode of God's presence changes. To explain this change let us use the following image.

The soul is like a deep ocean. During the active night of sense, God is like the sun that dances upon the surface of the waves. The soul is filled with joy, for the whole world seems to sparkle. The joy of doing God's will and loving one's neighbor is the bright atmosphere in which it lives and breathes. But one day, the sun is shrouded and the whole world turns gray. The waves become dull and dark. The soul's sprightliness wanes. Praying, practicing virtue, and responding to one's neighbor in love have become burdensome. God seems to be absent. However, only the mode of his presence has changed. God is no longer found on the surface of the waves because he is present on the bottom of the ocean, where the water is deep and still. John calls this gentle, quiet mode of God's presence *contemplation*.

Contemplation *is* God; he is present to the soul as gently as air rests on the palms of our hands (N.1.9.6). Since this is the case, the soul should no longer try to "think" about God during prayer, as it did when it prayed discursively; rather, the soul should rest in the awareness of God's presence. For "in this loving awareness the soul receives God's self-communication passively, just as people receive light passively without doing anything else but keeping their eyes open" (A.2.15.2).

Even though God's presence as contemplation should bring peace to the soul, it often creates distress. There are different reasons this happens. First, the cessation of consolation is a loss of pleasure. The soul no longer feels the joy it had experienced previously. Second, since the soul is unaware that the mode of God's presence has shifted to "the bottom of the ocean," it feels that something is wrong. The soul will often say to itself (and sometimes to others), "I'm not trying hard enough." In consequence, it will redouble its efforts to meditate discursively, which only makes matters worse. Third, an ignorant spiritual director will often confirm a soul in its misconception. "Directors will tell them they are falling back since they find no satisfaction or consolation as they previously did in the things of God. Such talk only doubles the trial of the poor soul" (A. Prol. 5). John calls this dry, confusing, and painful period the *passive night of sense*. It is a time of transition when the soul detaches itself from God's consoling presence and learns to adjust itself to God's contemplative presence.

As the soul ceases to try to regain its former consolation in prayer and gains insight into how God is now present to it, it realizes that its main task is to be attentive to God's gentle presence. During times of prayer, this means that individuals "must be content simply with a loving and peaceful attentiveness to God, and live without the concern, without the effort and without the desire to taste or feel Him" (N.1.10.4). Outside of prayer, the main tasks are to remain attentive and attuned to the gentle promptings of God's Spirit and to respond to the daily events of life in faith, hope, and love. This new mode of God's presence (contemplation) and the soul's receptivity and response to it John calls the *active night of the spirit*.

For all intents and purposes, the active night of the spirit is the spiritual path that we walk for the rest of our lives. The active night of sense, with its accompanying consolation, has often been referred to as the "honeymoon" period of our relationship with God. In contrast, the active night of the spirit has been compared to the day-in and day-out task of growing in knowledge and love of one's spouse, after the honeymoon is over. Over the years, a couple becomes attuned to one another. Each knows instinctively what the other is thinking and feeling and what he or she must do in order to love his or her mate. The same is true with the soul that is growing daily in its love for God. It becomes highly attuned to God's contemplative presence and acquires an instinctive knowledge of what it must say and do in order to grow in love of God and neighbor.

Even though John focuses on the difference between the way that God is present to the soul during the active night of sense and the active night of the spirit, this is not the most important difference between these two subdivisions of the dark night. The crucial difference lies in who is in control.

In the active night of sense, for the most part, we are in charge. We choose the ascetical exercises that we practice. We choose what we let go of. We choose how and when we pray. We choose what virtues we practice. This process of moral realignment and spiritual purification requires no special illumination from God. All the soul needs to do is to engage in ascetical practices that follow the dictates of reason, morality, and moderation. However, as the inflow of God's presence changes from consolation to contemplation, the soul becomes more receptive and responsive to God's voice. It relinquishes the lead. It becomes more willing to be instructed in love (N.2.5.1).

PASSIVE NIGHT OF THE SPIRIT

In the passive night of the spirit, the inflow of God intensifies; the guiding light of contemplation becomes a searing ray that "assails" the soul (N.2.5.5). The soul stands utterly exposed and is overwhelmed by what it sees. Stripped of all its rationalizations and defenses, the soul stands naked before its sinfulness and lack of integrity. In consequence, it feels utterly wretched and believes that God has abandoned it. However, in reality, God is more united to the soul than ever before. By continuing to love one's neighbor while it endures the experience of its poverty and the feeling that God is absent, the soul is transformed and united to God. John deals with the passive night of the spirit not in *The Ascent* but in his later prose commentary on *The Dark Night*.

SUBDIVISIONS OF THE DARK NIGHT AS STAGES

Are the subdivisions of the dark night sequential stages or do they occur simultaneously? Though this is a valid question, it is not a helpful one, for the question's either/or nature can lead us to believe that the subdivisions have to either be sequential or take place simultaneously. In fact, they are both. It would be more useful to ask the following questions: In what way can the subdivisions of the dark night be considered sequential stages? In what way do they overlap? Let us explore how both occur.

Why do most books written on St. John of the Cross present his schema of spiritual growth by means of the following stages? Stage 1: The active night of sense. Stage 2: The passive night of sense / The active night of the spirit. Stage 3: The passive night of the spirit. The answer is simple. In broad strokes, we see this schema in John's writings.

This schema is based upon common patterns in the spiritual life. For example, most souls at the beginning of the spiritual road experience the grace of "first fervor," which quickly wanes (active night of sense/passive night of sense). Likewise, it is a common experience that as a soul is faithful to the subtle promptings of the Spirit in daily life (the active night of the spirit), God will lead it into a deeper process of purification and transformation (the passive night of the spirit).

John holds that the above "stages" are predictable for many souls. He bases this belief not only on experience but also on how God works in the soul. "God perfects people gradually, according to their human nature" (A.2.17.4). God leads the soul through a step-by-step process of transformation (A.2.17.2). In short, God doesn't overwhelm the soul in the process of transformation but "disposes all things gently" (A.2.17.2). However, since *sense* and *spirit* form a "whole harmonious composite" (N.2.11.4), both parts of the soul are purified simultaneously. Furthermore, "one part is never adequately purged without the other" (N.2.3.1). In consequence, even though there is a certain sequence in the two purgations, they are not completely linear because both sense and spirit are purified at the same time.

BEGINNER, PROFICIENT, PERFECT

Besides his own fourfold schema of the dark night, John employs the traditional divisions of the spiritual life: the purgative way, the illuminative way, and the unitive way, with their corresponding types of souls: beginners, proficients, and perfects. It is important for us to understand how John uses these terms in his writings, for he employs them frequently.

John's term *beginner* can be misleading. It suggests a person who has just begun to embark on the spiritual road. However, John's beginners have already traveled several miles along the purgative way. They have established spiritual disciplines in their lives; they have progressed in overcoming vices; they are growing in the virtues; and they practice discursive prayer. In one sense, we are all beginners. For no matter how far we have "advanced," don't all of us struggle with the same vices year after year and find remaining faithful to our spiritual disciplines a daily challenge? This is but another example of why the "stages" of the spiritual life are not completely linear.

John does not spend much time writing about the life of beginners. Rather, his point of departure is at the time that God draws "them *out* of the state of beginners . . . and places them in the state of proficients"(N.1.1.1; italics added). John's starting point is not the beginning of the road but rather the transition point that he calls the *passive night of sense*. In short, John deals with beginners at the point where they cease being beginners.

Souls that have been drawn out of the state of beginners are called proficients. Like the word *beginner*, *proficient* can also be a misleading term. For in common usage, when we say that someone is proficient, we mean that he or she is an expert or he or she has mastered a certain skill. However, John's use of the word is derived from the Latin *proficiens*, meaning to go forward or to make progress.

There are similarities between beginners and proficients. Both are in need of purification, both struggle to overcome sin, and both strive to do the will of God. However, proficients are further along the road in these areas. They have a greater stability in their lives than do beginners. They have more control over their passions, guard themselves from mortal sin, and are more constant in the exercise of virtue. Proficients are more disposed to the enlightenment of divine grace than are beginners; thus, they are associated with what is called the *illuminative way*.

"Perfects" is another misleading term, for it gives the impression that John is writing of souls that are free from any fault or imperfection. However, this is not the case. For even souls in the "state of perfection" do not have a guarantee that they will not fall into sin. In this regard, St. Teresa of Avila, writing of souls that have reached the state of union with God, comments, "Nor should it pass through your minds that, since these souls have such determination and strong desires not to commit any imperfection for anything on earth, they fail to commit many imperfections, and even sins. Advertently, no:

for the Lord must give souls such as these very particular help against such a thing. I mean venial sins, for from what these souls can understand they are free from mortal sins, *although not immune*" (IC.7.4.3; italics added).

For John, "perfect" souls are those who have passed through the nights of sense and spirit and, thus, are deeply purified of their inordinate appetites. In consequence, while they are "not immune" to falling, they are less likely to do so because their wills have been transformed by grace.

These "perfect" souls tread the unitive way because they are deeply united to God by the theological virtues of faith, hope, and love. As a result of purification, their inner resistance to doing God's will has been all but eradicated. In consequence, they respond to God willingly, promptly, and wholeheartedly.

The progress of these three types of souls, corresponding to the purgative way, the illuminative way, and the unitive way, is described by Blessed Henry Suso's oft-quoted words: "A recollected person must be *unformed* of the creature (purgative way), become *informed* with Christ (illuminative way), and *transformed* into God (unitive way)" (italics added). Whether we are beginners, proficients, or perfects, all of us are being unformed and informed in the process of becoming transformed.

For Reflection

Is there something in my life that God is asking me to end? Is there something in my life that God is asking me to begin?

BOOK ONE

Appetite and Appetites

In *The Ascent of Mount Carmel,* John addresses a basic conflict that arises within all those who travel a spiritual path. We want to do the will of God, but we do not want to suffer. We want to grow in the love of God, but "[we] do *not want* to enter the dark night" (A. Prol. 3; italics added).

Such is the human condition; our wills are divided. Perhaps the truth of William Faulkner's claim that the only thing worth writing about is the human heart in conflict with itself lies in the fact that it is the only thing we can write about, for it is the universal condition of our unredeemed nature. We are divided creatures at odds with ourselves. As St. Paul writes, "I can will what is right, but I cannot do it. For I do not do the good I want, but the evil I do not want is what I do" (Rom 7:15–18).

We have the desire to do good but not the power. We have a desire to choose the good, but because of our wounded nature, we often lack the capacity to do so. We want to be happy, but we make choices that make us miserable. As the root of our misery, John calls our inordinate (*desorden*) appetites desires that are not ordered to our well-being and happiness.

To understand what John means by our *inordinate* appetites, we first need to understand that appetite (*apetito*) is not a pejorative word in his lexicon. *Apetito* is a synonym for hunger, drive, or desire. According to the Scholastic tradition of which

19

John is a part, desire is the drive at the core of our being that makes us seek God as our fulfillment.

The Scholastic would argue that there is a common thread in all of our strivings, a unity that harmonizes the complexity of all of our choices, a single desire that underlies all of our desires. In short, we seek the same thing in all things: happiness.

Happiness, as the Scholastics understood it, does not consist in "having fun," "feeling good," or any other fleeting pleasure or passing mood. It is a quality of soul that is obtained when one's deepest nature comes to fulfillment. The fulfillment of human nature, the Scholastics would argue, consists in being united to God, since we are made in God's image and likeness. In short, the object that will make us happy is determined by how we are made.

Furthermore, the Scholastics held that all of our desires have both a finite and an infinite dimension; they seek both an immediate and an ultimate object. For example, food is the immediate object of physical hunger, but hunger is expressive of our deepest hunger for God. Likewise, sexual desire is more than a physiological, psychological, and emotional drive to assuage the ache of separateness and to be united to another. It is also our longing to be united with the Other. It is within this understanding that every desire has both a finite and an infinite dimension that we can understand the nature of our inordinate desires; we seek to fulfill our infinite longing by means of a finite object, a creature.

CREATURES AS CRUMBS

John compares creatures to "crumbs that have fallen from God's table" (A.1.6.3). This is not a pejorative metaphor. It connotes that creatures are an overflow of God's bounty that drops down to us from above and serves to quicken our desire for God. John says as much in the *Spiritual Canticle*. Creatures are "like the crumbs given to someone who is famished" that serve to "increase the hunger and appetite [of the soul] to see God" (C.6.4). A creature "is like a messenger bringing the soul news of who God is" (C.6.4). Creatures are meant to whet our appetite for the Creator.

To comprehend the difference between the souls that John describes in *The Ascent* and those in *The Spiritual Canticle*, we must understand how they are similar. They are similar in that their reaction to creatures is the same. Since creatures give us a glimpse of God (e.g., God's goodness, beauty, etc.), they awaken our desire to see that which is still to be revealed. However, since creatures cannot fulfill the desire they evoke, they leave us pining for something more.

The difference lies in the response to the reaction that is evoked, a difference that constitutes the single most important choice in the spiritual life because it determines how we relate to the deepest desire of our hearts, our desire for God. The Bride in *The Spiritual Canticle* knows that creatures cannot satisfy her deepest longing and has accepted this fact. Consequently, she has chosen to suffer what it means to be human, to bear the inner ache and longing for that which cannot be fulfilled on this earth. It is a choice to bear the pain of incompleteness, a choice that refuses to satiate and anesthetize her heartfelt hunger with something less than God, and a choice not to seek the infinite in the finite.

Thus, we may say that our inordinate (*desorden*) appetites are attempts to fulfill the deepest and holiest longing of our heart in ways that will always end in frustration. Desire becomes disordered when we seek to satisfy the deepest longing of our heart with objects that cannot satisfy. This is why

John says that when we attempt to satisfy our deepest long-ing with creatures, we dig "leaking cisterns that cannot contain the water that slakes thirst"; they are "not one's proper food" (A.1.6.6). In short, our desire for God becomes disordered, not because our desire is evil but because the way we try to fulfill it just won't work.

The cruelest paradox of life is that an inordinate pursuit of happiness leads to misery. We can blindly stumble through life from delusion to delusion. "At last I have found it: the perfect mate, the ideal job, my dream house, the magical diet, and so forth." William F. Lynch calls this phenomenon the "Absolu-tizing Instinct," the father of hopeless dreams, who is forever making promises that he cannot keep.[1]

What happens to us over a lifetime when our inordinate pursuit of happiness leaves us wanting? John gives us a sober-ing answer. He says that the chief characteristic (*propiedad*), which can be translated as "particular quality" or "personality trait," is that we become "dissatisfied (*descontento*) and bitter (*desabrido*)" (A.1.6.3).

Descontento means to be discontented. If we are always comparing everything in life to some unrealistic standard of perfection, everything will disappoint us and nothing will satisfy us. This discontent can sour our soul and make us bitter on life. People who are chronically discontented begin to blame the whole world for their misery. "It is every-one else's fault that I'm miserable. Life has dealt me a rot-ten hand. Nothing has ever gone my way. People have done me wrong." In Dante's *Inferno*, as the souls of the damned are about to enter hell, they spew forth a litany of blame. "They blaspheme God, their parents, their time on earth, the race of Adam, and the day and the hour and the place and the seed and the womb that gave them birth."[2] This is why they are there; they have abdicated responsibility for their own choices.

This is a frightening image of what we can become—resentful people who have grown bitter on life. John says that on the spiritual path there is no standing still: we are either progressing or regressing; we are either becoming conformed to God's gracious will or becoming deformed. The choice is ours.

> *For*
> *Reflection*
>
> Where in my life is my quest for happiness making me miserable?

Discontentment

When I was in high school, I fell in love with classical music. My favorite works were the symphonies and concertos of the Romantic composers: Beethoven, Mendelssohn, Schubert, Schumann, and Brahms. Several years ago, when I read that *The Late String Quartets of Beethoven* were considered his most mature works and regarded as some of the most deeply spiritual music that had ever been composed, I purchased a recording of the quartets. I expected to be deeply stirred by Beethoven's quartets as I had always been by his symphonies, but I was sorely disappointed. I could not perceive the spiritual depth that they contained. The music sounded abstract, dissonant, and harsh. In short, the quartets clashed with my aesthetic taste. However, taste was not the only cause of my disappointment; the quartets deprived me of what I had wanted to hear: music that would touch my emotions.

In chapter 5 of book one of *The Ascent*, John describes a similar experience. Using the sojourn of the Hebrews in the desert as a metaphor for the spiritual life, John says that the Hebrews were unable to perceive the sweetness contained in the manna because they were still craving the savory food they had left behind in Egypt. "This bread of angels is disagreeable to the palate of anyone who wants to taste human food. . . . The people, discontented (*no conviene*) with that simple (*sencillo*) food, requested and craved meat. . . . If spiritual persons knew how much spiritual good and abundance they lose by not attempting to raise their appetites above childish things . . . they would discover in this simple (*sencillo*) spiritual food the savor (*gusto*) of all things. They did not perceive the taste of every other food that was contained in the manna, because their appetite was not centered on this manna alone" (A.1.5.3–4).

In these few words, John describes one of the main sources of our misery. The Spanish word that is translated discontented (*no conviene*) refers to a situation in which nothing coincides, corresponds, or suits what we want. In this regard, there is no upper limit to the amount of unhappiness that we can inflict upon ourselves. The more that we demand that life be tailored to our desires, the more wretched we become. Like the Hebrews in the desert, we become discontented when we are unable to find joy in what God sets before us. Life becomes insipid when we are unable to perceive the nourishing presence of God who is "the savor (*gusto*) of all things." Since *gusto* can be translated as pleasure, delight, or contentment, John seems to be saying that souls who seek their happiness in God alone will find delight in *all things* because they will be content with what God provides.

It is instructive that the root of the word happiness is *hap*, meaning "to happen." This suggests that happiness is our capacity to find joy in what is happening. For most of us, being happy is future tense. We are caught up in a mad pursuit of some illusive goal that is forever just beyond our reach. We are blinded "like a fish dazzled by the light" chasing a glittering lure (A.1.8.3).

For
Reflection

What inordinate desires or pursuits are preventing me from savoring the simple joys of daily life?

Denial of Gratification

Chapter 3 of book one of *The Ascent* is highly susceptible to rationalization. First, it tells a truth that all of us want to avoid: to enter the dark night we must deprive ourselves "of the gratification (*gusto*) of the soul's appetites in all things" (A.1.3.1). In short, we have to modify and, in some instances, completely deprive ourselves of pleasurable experiences.

Just thinking of embarking upon this desert road is enough to make us depressed. So, how do we deal with this uncomfortable truth? After telling us that we must mortify our inordinate appetites, John says that "we are not discussing the *mere lack of things*; this lack will not divest the soul if it *craves* for all these objects. We are dealing with the denudation of the soul's appetites and gratification" (A.1.3.4; italics added). In short, John is saying that our attachments reside in the will.

We can easily use our powers of rationalization to twist the meaning of this truth. We can give it the following interpretation: "Since John says that we are dealing with not a mere lack of things but rather our desire for things, then we don't have to give up using objects as long as we are not attached to them." John would agree with this statement. However, he would also point out that the means by which our appetite becomes detached from things is by mortifying it. In other words, we actually have to modify or deprive ourselves of the use of objects in order to become detached from them.

For Reflection | Do I have an inordinate attachment to some object or pleasure that God is asking me to change or modify? Is rationalization preventing me from doing so?

Harms

Thomas Hardy once described a tragic figure as someone who awakens too late to the destructive consequences of indulging his passions, prejudices, and ambitions. Such was the case with the prodigal son as he sat in the mire of the consequences of his choices. It was only when he was starving in a foreign land that he came to his senses and decided to return to his father's house. How often have we been in a similar situation? How often has the self-inflicted misery of our choices been a motivating force for change?

In chapters 6 through 10 of book one of *The Ascent*, John sets before us the self-inflicted misery, damage, or harm (*dañar*, to hurt, to damage) that follows in the wake of indulging our inordinate appetites. John mentions two types of harms: *privative* and *positive*.

PRIVATIVE HARM

The deepest harm that inordinate desires can inflict upon a soul is the privative harm, the loss of desire for God. In attempting to explain this loss, John compares it to a change in our very nature or substantial form (A.1.6.2–3). In Scholastic philosophy, *form* distinguishes and differentiates one kind of being from another. For example, the form of a dog is everything that constitutes "dogginess"; it is what makes a dog a dog as distinct from a cat, a chipmunk, or an aardvark. The form is the element in a creature (that can be described but never clearly defined) that makes it a member of a particular class or species. Furthermore, every species has an innate drive toward self-actualization, an inborn desire that seeks its proper good or fulfillment. The form of humankind is the soul, and the proper good that they seek as creatures made in the image and likeness of God is to be united with God.

Thus, John is saying that desire is the life-organizing principle that regulates our lives and determines what we seek. And whenever our desire changes, such a radical alteration takes place within us that it can be compared to a creature whose form has changed.

Consider the following scenario. Joe and Pete were good friends in high school. They palled around together and shared the same values. They both wanted to do something with their lives that would make a difference in the world. After graduation, Joe joined the Peace Corps and served in Uganda for four years. On returning to the United States, he became a social worker, and for the next twenty years dedicated himself to eradicating poverty in Washington, D.C. Pete, on the other hand, obtained an MBA and landed a lucrative job on Wall Street.

At their thirty-fifth class reunion, they met one another for the first time since graduation. As they talked through the night, it became apparent to Joe that Pete was no longer the person he had known in high school. Everything that Pete said was in terms of profit and loss. Increasing sales, undercutting the competition, widening his company's profit margin, striking the best package for early retirement, and getting the best rates for a loan to purchase a new house in the suburbs defined his life's goal.

That night, when Joe was lying in bed, he thought to himself, "Pete's not the person I knew in high school. He is a different person." This is obviously metaphorical language, for Pete was the same person. However, since the whole orientation of Pete's life had undergone such a radical change, it was as if he were a different person. This illustrates John's teaching. Namely, when a person's life-organizing desire changes, it changes the person in such a radical way that it is almost as if he or she has become someone else. John is suggesting that since our desire for God is at the core of our nature, if we deform our desire for God, in some sense, we change our form.

We find an example of this transformation in Dickens's *A Christmas Carol*, where Scrooge's fiancée, Belle, breaks off her engagement to Scrooge. She says to him, "All your hopes have merged into the hope of being beyond the chance of [the world's] sordid reproach. I have seen your nobler aspirations fall off one by one, until the master passion, Gain, engrosses you. . . . Your own feeling tells you that *you were not what you are*. . . . [You now live] in a changed nature, in an altered spirit, in another atmosphere of life, in another Hope as its great end. . . . I release you, with a full heart, for the love of him *you once were*" (italics added).[3]

We all know by experience that when we are obsessed with an object, person, or project, we become oblivious to everything else. Our consciousness becomes so consumed and our minds so absorbed in our pursuit that we become deaf and blind to the world around us, even to our loved ones. The privative harm of our inordinate appetites deprives us of the light of reason and constricts our desire and capacity to love.

For Reflection

What inordinate attachment in my life produces these effects? What behaviors do I need to change in order to begin to heal the privative harm that my attachment is doing in my life?

Positive Harms

The specific effects that flow from the privative harm John calls the positive (*positivo*) harms. They "weary, torment, darken, defile [the soul]" (A.1.6.5).

Weary (A.1.6)

The Petulant Child and the Covetous Treasure Hunter (A.1.6.6)

In Leo Tolstoy's novel *Anna Karenina*, Count Vronsky falls in love with Anna and pursues her relentlessly, believing she will confer ecstatic happiness upon him. After convincing Anna to leave her husband, Vronsky was happy because now he possessed the object of his desire. However, he was happy only for a while.

> Vronsky, meanwhile, in spite of the complete realization of what he had so long desired, was not perfectly happy. He soon felt that the realization of his desires gave him no more than a grain of sand out of the mountain of happiness he had expected. It showed him the mistake men make in picturing to themselves happiness as the realization of their desires. For a time after joining his life to hers . . . he had felt all the delight of freedom in general of which he had known nothing before, and of freedom in his love—and he was content, but not for long. He was soon aware that there was springing up in his heart a desire for desires—*ennui*. Without conscious intention he began to clutch at every passing caprice, taking it for a desire and an object. . . . And just as the hungry stomach accepts every object it can get, hoping to find nourishment in it, Vronsky quite unconsciously clutched first at politics, then at new books, and then at

> pictures. . . . [Vronsky decided to try his hand at paint-
> ing] and concentrated upon it the unoccupied mass of
> desires which demanded satisfaction.[4]

We see in Vronsky the twofold weariness caused by our inordinate appetites: they drive us mad in our pursuit and leave us
empty in our attainment. This twofold weariness is illustrated
in John's description of a lover. "Just as a lover is wearied and
depressed when on a longed-for day his opportunity is frustrated, so is the soul wearied and tired of all its appetites *and
their fulfillment*, because the fulfillment only causes more hunger and emptiness" (A.1.6.6; italics added).

This twofold weariness is also manifested in John's images
of the petulant child and the covetous treasure hunter. Both
images convey the same truth about the weariness engendered
by our inordinate appetites but emphasize different aspects of
it. John begins his treatment of the harm of weariness with
the following statement: "It is plain that the appetites are wea-
risome (*cansan*) and tiring (*fatigans*)" (A.1.6.6). While *cansan*
and *fatigans* are synonyms, their meanings can vary, depending
on the context in which they are used. *Cansan* can express the
exhaustion that accompanies boredom. This aspect of weariness is emphasized in John's image of the petulant child: "[Our
appetites] resemble little children, restless, and hard to please,
always whining to their mother for this thing or that, and
never satisfied" (A.1.6.6.).

On the other hand, *fatigans* emphasizes the exhaustion
that is the result of hard work. This meaning is emphasized
in the image of the covetous treasure hunter. "Just as anyone
who digs covetously for a treasure grows tired and exhausted,
so does anyone who strives to satisfy the appetites' demands
become wearied and fatigued" (A.1.6.6.).

Together, the images of the covetous treasure hunter and the bored child form a sort of "wheel of weariness." The weariness of boredom follows upon the weariness of pursuit in a never-ending cycle. Once our inordinate appetites obtain the object of their pursuit, they are content, but only for a while. Soon, an inner restlessness takes hold of us, and a new pursuit begins.

We are often like Count Vronsky. After he had won Anna, his old restlessness returned. He attempted to anesthetize his restlessness by some new diversion. "Vronsky's interest in painting did not last long. . . . With his characteristic decision he simply ceased working at painting."[5]

Restlessness is not the problem. It is an experience of our deepest desire for God. Our hearts are restless, and they will not rest until they rest in God. The problem is that we try to fill up our restlessness with diversions that do not nourish our soul. And like Vronsky, we become "distracted from distraction by distraction."[6]

Leaking Cisterns (A.1.6.6)

We can understand why Vronsky continued his weary pursuit to satisfy his inordinate appetites. There were moments when they were temporarily satisfied. Such moments sustained his pursuit. However, our inordinate appetites can be so strong that we will continue our pursuit in the face of utter exhaustion, failure, and futility. We have an example of this in Ray Bradbury's novel *Fahrenheit 451*, when Montag, the protagonist, reflects upon an event of his childhood. "Once as a child he had sat upon a yellow dune by the sea in the middle of the blue and hot summer day, trying to fill a sieve with sand, because some cruel cousin had said, 'Fill this sieve and you'll get a dime!' And the faster he poured, the faster it sifted through with a hot whispering. His hands were tired, the sand was boiling, the sieve was empty. Seated there in the midst of July, without a sound, he felt the tears move down his cheeks."[7]

Montag's attempt to fill the sieve with sand illustrates the irrational blindness at the heart of our inordinate appetites. His desire for the dime blinded him to the utter futility of his pursuit, which in the end left him utterly weary and empty.

Likewise, John presents us with a similar image of futility and weariness. "For after all, one digs leaking cisterns that cannot contain the water that slakes thirst . . . and his soul is [left] empty" (Is 29:8; A.1.6.6). John's image of the leaking cistern presents us with a frightening aspect of our inordinate appetites, namely, that we will pursue an object beyond reason and beyond hope.

> *For*
> *Reflection*
>
> A "wheel of weariness" is triggered when we are like a petulant child, whose restlessness can never be satisfied. Is there an illusionary pursuit of happiness, driven by an inordinate desire, which has created a "wheel of weariness" in my life?

Torment (A.1.7)

In Dostoevsky's novel *Crime and Punishment*, Raskolnikov has a desperate need to prove to himself that he is a superior human being who is not subject to the constraints of conscience. He becomes obsessed with the idea that he should be able to commit a brutal crime without feeling guilt or remorse. He is unaware of how much he is being brutalized by his obsession until one day he has a dream.

In the dream, Raskolnikov is seven years old. He is in his hometown. One evening, as he and his father are walking in the countryside, they pass by a tavern, in front of which is a cart attached to a gaunt horse. A drunken crowd comes out of the tavern and climbs into the cart. Mikolka, the owner of the cart, begins to whip the horse, but the horse is unable to pull its heavy load. Mikolka continues to whip the horse while the passengers beat the horse about its head. In rage, Mikolka climbs off the cart and strikes the horse on its spine and head with a crowbar. The horse falls to its knees and keels over dead. As Raskolnikov watches this brutal scene, tears stream down his cheeks. He runs up to the horse and kisses and caresses it. Upon awakening, Raskolnikov feels a deep sense of relief. "He felt he had cast off that fearful burden that had so long been weighing him down, and all at once there was a sense of relief and peace of soul. . . . It was as though an abscess that had been forming . . . in his heart had suddenly broken. He was free from that spell, that sorcery, that obsession!"[8]

Raskolnikov's dream revealed to him how brutal and merciless was his obsession. However, it also invited him to have compassion upon himself. This is symbolized at the end of the dream when Raskolnikov weeps over the dead horse. Psychiatrist Karen Horney, commenting upon this scene writes, "And from the depth of his being emerged a profound compassion for himself over what he was doing to himself. Having thus experienced his true feelings, he felt more at one with himself after the dream and decided against the killing."[9]

Are we any different than Raskolnikov? Are we not driven by some fiction of the mind, obsessed by a belief that some object will confer upon us lasting peace or happiness, be it wealth, power, prestige, beauty, or the esteem of others? Do we not mercilessly whip ourselves to acquire the reputation of being competent, intelligent, knowledgeable, reliable, or virtuous?

In writing of how our inordinate appetites torment us, John uses an image similar to the one we find in Raskolnikov's dream. "Just as a peasant, covetous of the desired harvest, goads and torments the ox that pulls the plow, so concupiscence, in order to attain the object of its longing, afflicts the one who lives under the yoke of its appetites" (A.1.7.1).

John is drawing our attention to the sheer brutality of what we do to ourselves, the utter disregard that we have for our own welfare when we are goaded by a disordered desire. How often have we felt driven like a beast of burden and have said to ourselves, "This madness has got to stop"? But our best efforts are often outmatched by the brutal and tenacious strength of our inordinate appetites. What accounts for the incredible strength of our inordinate appetites is a twofold dynamic inherent in the nature of our appetites.

The Scholastic concept of appetite (*appetitus*) is not equivalent to the English word *desire* because desire simply connotes a movement toward an object. The Latin word *appetitus* contains a movement both toward and away from an object; there is an approach/avoidance or attraction/aversion dynamic in *appetitus*.

The peasant who goads the ox is driven by not only the desire for food but also the fear of starvation. When we run toward a good, we simultaneously run away from an evil. What we seek to obtain is inexorably fused to what we seek to avoid. Thus, the strength of any appetite lies in the combination and interrelationship of the four natural passions of hope and joy (attraction), and sorrow and fear (aversion). For example, the desire to be special belies the fear of being ordinary. The craving for power masks the dread of helplessness and the humiliation of being subservient. The pursuit of fame and prestige cloaks the terror of insignificance, and the hoarding of possessions quells the anxiety of destitution. This twofold dynamic of appetite is also operative in our most basic drives. We crave food, drink, and sex not only for the pleasure that they afford but also for the hunger, thirst, tension, loneliness, and emptiness that they assuage.

In short, our inordinate appetites are doubly addictive and reinforcing, for they provide pleasure and protect us from pain. They are habit forming because we tend to repeat behaviors that are rewarding. Each time we gratify an inordinate appetite, its strength increases because the bond between indulgence and its consequent reward is strengthened. The brute strength of our inordinate appetites is symbolized by John's metaphors of being tied to a rack with cords or chained to a millstone (A.1.7.2). In short, we are captured, held prisoner, and tormented by the object of our pursuit.

John's treatment of the torment that our inordinate appetites inflict upon us parallels Raskolnikov's dream. John begins by presenting us with images that are frightening in their brutality but concludes with an invitation to self-compassion. By quoting the prophet Isaiah ("Come to the waters") and St. Matthew's Gospel ("Come to me all you who labor and are heavily burdened"), John reminds us that God is merciful and compassionate and desires to heal our tormented souls (A.1.7.4). Just as from the depth of Raskolnikov's soul emerged a profound sense of compassion for himself, so too, does there dwell within us a compassionate God who invites us to relinquish our madness and to come home to ourselves.

For Reflection	In what ways do my inordinate appetites brutalize me? How is God inviting me to give up the madness that is engendered by my inordinate appetites?

Darken (A.1.8)

The Clouded Mirror (*A.1.8.1*)

When we know that what we are doing is against God's will, we feel either guilty or ill at ease with ourselves. If we do not change our behavior, we will attempt to rationalize it. However, rationalization only blunts our awareness that what we are doing is wrong. It does not blot it out. This is the state of soul that John describes by the following images: "The third kind of harm the appetites bring upon a person is blindness and darkness. Vapors make the air murky and are a hindrance to the bright sunshine; a cloudy mirror does not clearly reflect a person's countenance; so too muddy water reflects only a hazy image of one's features" (A.1.8.1).

Our inordinate appetites dim the light of reason; they do not extinguish it. The murky air only hinders the sunlight; it does not eclipse it. A cloudy mirror reflects a person's countenance but not clearly. Though muddy water reflects a person's features, it provides only an image that is hazy.

John is describing a painful state of blindness engendered by our inordinate appetites. Since the soul does not have the capacity to completely block out of consciousness its true condition before God, it can never be at peace with itself.

The Moth (*A.1.8.3*)

In George Eliot's dark fantasy *The Lifted Veil*, Latimer, a young clairvoyant, is irresistibly drawn to Bertha Grant. He is so captivated by Bertha that he marries her, although his clairvoyant powers have made him aware that she will poison him.

> The tumult of mind into which I was thrown by this hideous vision made me ill for several days. . . . Yet such is

the madness of the human heart under the influence of its immediate desires, I felt a wild hell-braving joy that Bertha was to be mine. . . . I trembled under her touch; I felt the witchery of her presence; I yearned to be assured of her love. The fear of poison is feeble against the sense of thirst. . . . The future, even when brought within the compass of feeling by a vision that made me shudder, had still no more than the force of an idea, compared with the present emotion. . . . An insight at war with passion . . . the powerlessness of ideas before the might of impulse . . . once passed into memory, were mere ideas—pale shadows that beckoned in vain.[10]

Eliot is describing what may be termed *wide-eyed* blindness. Latimer is fully conscious of the deadly fate that awaits him if he marries Bertha, but this realization is not a deterrent, for it has only "the force of an idea." The passion of the moment is so strong that it eviscerates any consideration of future consequence. Or as John puts it, "A light set directly in front of the visual faculty blinds this faculty so that it fails to see the light farther away" (A.1.8.3).

The failure to see the distant light is not a lack of awareness. It is the result of being so absorbed in the passion of the moment that we disregard the consequence of a self-destructive course of action. This is the reality symbolized by John's image of the moth that flies wide-eyed into a flame. "A moth is not helped much by its eyes because, blinded in its desire for the beauty of light, it will fly directly into a bonfire" (A.1.8.3).

We all have our fatal attractions. No matter how often we are burnt by fire, it seems that we are powerless to stay away from the source of our misery. And against our better judgment, we are drawn back over and over again. You would think that we would learn from our mistakes.

John tells us that desire "dulls" the memory (A.1.8.2); that is, in the heat of the moment, we can recall the painful consequences of past choices, but those memories have no more force than that of a vague idea. Our inordinate appetites encapsulate us in the present moment so that we ignore the painful lessons of the past and become heedless of future danger.

The Fisherman's Lure (A.1.8.3)

"Those who feed on their appetites are like a fish dazzled by a light that so darkens it that the fisherman's lure cannot be seen" (A.1.8.3). The psychological and spiritual dynamics of blindness contained in this image are similar to those that we discussed in our previous reflection, namely, that the pursuit of our inordinate appetites darkens the intellect, weakens the will, and dulls the memory (A.1.8.2). However, this image contains an added dimension: it is only after the bait has been swallowed that our eyes are opened. This is because "these evils do not unmask themselves *at the moment* the appetite is being satisfied, since the pleasure of the moment is an obstacle to this. Yet *sooner or later* the harmful effects will certainly be felt" (A.1.12.5; italics added).

Sometimes it is sooner. In fact, often it happens immediately after the appetite is satiated. This frequently happens when the appetite is savage in strength. This truth is expressed in Shakespeare's Sonnet 129.

> The expense of spirit in a waste of shame
>
> Is lust in action: and till action, lust
>
> Is perjur'd, murderous, bloody, full of blame,
>
> savage, extreme, rude, cruel, not to trust;

Enjoy'd no sooner but despised straight;

Past reason hunted; and no sooner had,

Past reason hated, as a swallow'd bait,

On purpose laid to make the taker mad:

Mad in pursuit and in possession so;

Had, having, and in quest, to have extreme;

A bliss in proof—and prov'd, a very woe;

Before, a joy propos'd; behind a dream.

All this the world well knows; yet none knows well

to shun the heaven that leads men to this hell.[11]

(italics added)

While the explicit content of this sonnet is sexual lust, its underlying subject matter is the vicissitudes of desire. It is about desire "had [past], having [present], and in quest [future]." And in each phase, the experience is "extreme." The pursuit is "savage"; the possession is "heaven," and the remembrance is "hell."

At other times, it is only long after we have indulged our inordinate appetites that we recognize their harmful effects. In this regard, St. Augustine, writing of greed for temporal goods, says the following: "Such delight, however, is blindness and utter misery, for it ensnares the soul all the more and leads it on to worse afflictions. The fish is delighted, too, when, failing to notice the hook, it devours the bait. But, when the fisherman begins to draw his line, first the fish's inner parts are dislocated; after that it is dragged to its destruction, away from all the pleasure that its joy in the bait had brought it. So it is with all who imagine they are happy with temporal goods. They have swallowed the hook and wander aimlessly about with it. The time will come for them to experience how much anguish they have devoured in their greediness."[12] We all know the truth contained in Augustine's image. Often in life, it is only long after we have indulged our inordinate appetites that their destructive effects become manifest.

For Reflection — We all have our fatal attractions. What do I believe God is instructing me to do in order to protect myself against them? Do I have a desire that makes me pursue something with a savage intensity that overwhelms me with guilt and shame the moment it is satisfied? Have I ever awakened to the harmful consequences that an inordinate habit has had on my life over time? Have I ever considered that this realization is God's merciful invitation to change?

Defile (A.1.9)

On Pentecost Sunday, May 12, 1972, Hungarian-born Australian geologist Lazlo Toth dashed past the guards at St. Peter's Basilica in Rome, vaulted over a balustrade, and dealt fifteen hammer blows to Michelangelo's marble masterpiece, the Pietà. The art world was stunned and stood in horror. But wasn't this an overreaction? After all, the damage was not extensive; the statue's left arm was severed at the elbow, and the nose and left eye were chipped. A bottle of Elmer's glue, a little restorative work, and things would be as good as new.

Such a glib reaction is an expression of ignorance and blindness. The amount of damage is not at issue but rather what was damaged. For when an object of immense beauty is marred, even by one unsightly mark, the effect is devastating. If the art world's reaction of horror in the face of the damage inflicted upon Michelangelo's Pietà is justified, how much more justified is such a reaction when God's masterpiece, the human soul, made in the divine image and likeness, is marred in any degree?

We find such a reaction in Oscar Wilde's novel *The Picture of Dorian Gray*. At the beginning of the story, Dorian Gray, an exceptionally handsome young man, has his portrait painted. It so captures the beauty of his youth that he begins to weep because he knows that as he grows older, his portrait will remind him of his fading youth. Dorian utters a mad wish that he would stay young forever and that his portrait would age and become a portrait of his soul. His wish becomes a reality.

One night, several weeks after making this wish, Dorian cruelly breaks off his engagement to Sibyl Vane. When he arrives home, he notices that a slight alteration has occurred in his portrait.

There was a touch of cruelty in the mouth. . . . There were no signs of any change when he looked into the actual painting, and yet there was no doubt that the whole expression had altered. . . . He had uttered a mad wish that he himself might remain young, and the portrait grow old; that the canvas bear the burden of his passions and sins. Surely his wish had not been fulfilled. Yet there was the picture before him with the touch of cruelty in the mouth. . . . [The portrait] was watching him, with its beautiful and marred face and its cruel smile . . . the visible emblem of his conscience. . . . He got up from his chair, and drew a large screen right in front of the portrait, shuddering as he glanced at it. "How horrible."[13]

Dorian's reaction of horror is due to his realization that a touch of cruelty has marred his entire face. He realizes that his one act of cruelty has altered his soul, or as John expresses this reality, "[Just as] strokes of soot would ruin a perfect and extraordinarily beautiful portrait, so too inordinate appetites defile and dirty the soul, in itself a perfect and extremely beautiful image of God" (A.1.9.1).

The metaphor of sin as defilement contains a basic truth about human nature, namely, that every experience leaves its imprint upon the soul. Every encounter with the created order deposits a residue that is recorded in memory and embedded in our physiology. Just as our bodies can be infected if exposed to germs, so too can our souls be infected if they are exposed to certain stimuli.

John's main point is as follows: if we are influenced by merely being exposed to or touched by something, how much more are we impacted when we touch something with our will in the heat of desire? We need to keep in mind that John is writing about the harms that our choices inflict upon our souls: "The voluntary appetites bring on all these evils" (A.1.12.6). Like Dorian Gray, each of us is in the process of painting a self-portrait in which every choice we make is a brushstroke.

For Reflection	Every choice I make is a brushstroke that I paint on the portrait of my soul. What daily choices do I make that contribute to either the beauty or defilement of my self-portrait?

Weaken (A.1.10)

F. Scott Fitzgerald's autobiographical story *Babylon Revisited* is about a recovering alcoholic named Charlie Wales, who is struggling to get back on his feet after a lifetime of dissipation. One night, as Charlie is walking down a street in Paris, he hears sounds of his old dissipated existence coming from the bars. He is arrested with the realization of the nature of his former life. "All the catering to vice and waste was on an utterly childish scale, and he suddenly realized the meaning of the word 'dissipate'—to dissipate into thin air; *to make nothing out of something*" (italics added).[14]

When we hear the word dissipation, people like Charlie Wales may come to our mind, for it has frequently been associated with people who have squandered their lives by overindulgence or recklessness. However, all of us can "make nothing out of something" by frittering away our lives on innocuous trifles. This is John's point in chapters 10 and 11 of book one of *The Ascent*.

To understand the tragic poignancy of these chapters, we need to keep in mind John's original audience: Carmelite nuns and friars (A. Prol. 9). In short, men and women who have been called by God to a vocation to grow in love of God and neighbor in community life. It is within this perspective that we should read John's comments: A "will . . . divided among trifles becomes weaker than if it were completely fixed on one object" (A.1.10.1). In chapter 11, John gives the following list of trifling habits: "Some examples of these habitual imperfections are: the common habit of being very talkative; a small attachment one never really desires to conquer, for example, to a person, to clothing, to a book or a cell, or to the way food is prepared, and to other trifling conversations and little satisfactions in tasting, knowing, and hearing things, and so on. Any of these habitual imperfections to which there is attachment is as harmful to progress in virtue as the daily commission of many other imperfections and sporadic venial sins that do not result from a bad habit. These latter will not hinder a person as much as will the attachment to something" (A.1.11.4).

When I first read this passage, I asked myself, "Is John serious? These are peccadilloes! How could he assign so much importance to trivialities?" I think John might respond to my puzzlement with the following: "Marc, you're right. The things that I mention are trivial in nature, but they are the very things out of which we fashion a lifestyle and in which we invest enormous amounts of time and energy. That's where the tragedy resides." The tragedy of being addicted to trivialities is that our lives become trivial. Let's explore such a possibility as illustrated in the life of St. Teresa of Avila:

When St. Teresa reflected upon one of the great crossroads in her life, namely, her decision to leave the convent of the Incarnation in order to found a new way of religious life, she wrote the following: "Yet since . . . I was perfectly content in the house in which I was because it was very much to my liking and the cell in which I lived was just what I wanted, I was still delaying" (L.32.10). As ludicrous as it may sound, Teresa's great reform may have never taken place because the décor of her cell was to her liking. But is this really so far-fetched? Teresa was forty-eight years old when she decided to leave the Incarnation. She had lived there all of her adult life and was settled in her ways.

How often has our unwillingness or inability to part with a small creature comfort that has taken root in our lives stood in the way of enterprises of great pitch and moment? Over how many areas of our lives have we hung a "Do Not Disturb" sign because we have become entrenched in some trivial ritual or daily routine? It is so easy to slide into a rut of indolence but so difficult to climb out of it.

Besides attachments to creature comforts such as "to clothing, to a book or a cell, or to the way food is prepared," and so on, John gives attention to our habitual attachments in the area of interpersonal exchange: "the common habit of being very talkative . . . and other trifling conversations" (A.1.11.4). In dealing with this category of habitual attachments, we need to keep John's original audience in mind, Carmelite nuns and friars, that is, people who live and work in close quarters together—in short, a situation where people are apt to get on one another's nerves and become embroiled in factions and gossipy cliques.

John was well aware of the dynamics of communal living, of how relationships are easily formed by a mutual gripe or grievance. He knew the all-too-common temptations of backbiting and mean-spirited gossip that can run rampant in a monastery or cloister and how addictive such spleen-venting behaviors can become.

At the beginning of *The Way of Perfection*, St. Teresa says she is going to write about temptations that "little attention is paid to," because they are "common, small temptations" (W. Prol.). This is one of the reasons "the *common* habit of being very talkative" is so dangerous. Common habits are behaviors that have become so habitual that we do them automatically. They have become so second nature to us that we no longer pay any attention to them; they have drifted outside the realm of self-reflection.

So how do we become aware of the common habits of which we are unaware? Let me offer one suggestion. Pay attention to your overreactions when one of your routines is ruptured or when something isn't done exactly the way you want it to be done. If your emotional reaction is disproportionate to the event, if you are bent out of shape by any little monkey wrench that is thrown into your well-oiled plans, then suspect that an inordinate attachment is present.

John compares his list of "trivial" attachments to a thin thread tied to a bird's leg that prevents it from flying. He says that even though such threads are easier to break than thick cords, they nevertheless hold the bird earthbound. The tragedy that is implied is that something so slight can hold us back from living a fuller life in God's grace.

Finally, our trivial attachments are insidious because they are very susceptible to our rationalizations. It is easy to make light of them and never consider the spiritual damage that they do. A thread may be thin, but if we cannot break it, then it is stronger than we are. And "[we] become as little as the things [we] love" (A.1.4.8).

For Reflection

There are many trivial things in our lives that are neither sinful nor immoral but nevertheless consume an inordinate amount of our time and energy. Consider one behavior you feel God is inviting you to modify. In John's list of habitual imperfections, he seems to put an emphasis on our habits of interpersonal exchange ("being very talkative . . . trifling conversations . . . satisfactions in knowing and hearing things"). Perhaps he was thinking of St. James's statement that the tongue could be a whole "world of iniquity" (Jas 3:6). Has a habit of gossip, backbiting, or maligning crept into my life at home, at work, or with friends?

The Threshold of Consent

All day long, objects of desire show up at the doorstep of our lives. Which ones we admit and which ones we turn away determine the creatures we are becoming. The fundamental choice of what gains access to our lives begins in our minds. "The threshold of consent," to use Dante's term, is where we stand all day long.[15]

The threshold of consent is the moment when a desire presents itself to the conscious mind and the will becomes inclined toward it. These embryonic stirrings of desire John calls "first movements." "The first movements are the entrances and thresholds of the soul" (C.18.8).

When these first movements arrive at the threshold of consciousness in the form of temptations, John says that they do the soul no harm if we resist them entrance. In so doing, they become the occasion of growing in virtue. "Insofar as one resists them, one wins strength, purity, comfort, and many blessings" (A.1.12.6).

This is a very important perspective to keep in mind when struggling with temptation. The "passion and disturbance [that temptations] momentarily cause *make it seem* that one is being defiled and blinded, such is *not the case*; rather, they occasion the opposite good effects" (A.1.12.6; italics added).

John is telling us not to be blind to the good that God is doing in our souls when we are being tempted.

There is no one reason that resisting temptation can make us feel defiled. Sometimes it is because the emotions or passions that accompany temptations (anger, lust, fear, etc.) cause a chemical change in our bodies. At other times, we can feel guilty just because we have been tempted.

While John is very insistent that we should be vigilant in resisting the first movements of temptation, he is also aware of the danger of feeling guilty about every thought, feeling, and impulse that shows up at the doorstep of our mind. Perhaps this danger is what John had in mind when he gave the following advice to one of his directees: "Do not confess scruples or first movements" (L.28).

As a confessor, I have noticed that many penitents are very precise in knowing the number of times that they have given in to a temptation. But when asked how often they have resisted the same temptation, they are at a loss to say. Such a lopsided knowledge of our spiritual life is both dangerous and tragic. First, it is dangerous because we can become discouraged, or as St. Teresa puts it, we "never get out of the mire of our miseries" (IC.1.2.10). Second, by focusing too much upon ourselves, we can become blind to God's grace operating in our lives.

For Reflection In the midst of struggling against temptation, have I ever thought to thank God for the grace that enables me to struggle?

To Exit Is to Enter

After having painted a sobering portrait of the havoc that we wreak upon ourselves by inordinately indulging our appetites, John offers us "counsels and methods" on how to overcome our misery by entering the dark night. Chapter 13 begins as follows: "Some counsels are in order now that the individual may both know the way of entering this night and be able to do so. It should be understood, consequently, that a person ordinarily enters this night of sense in two ways: active and passive. The active way, which will be the subject of the following counsels, comprises what one can do and does by oneself to enter this night" (A.1.13.1).

To understand this passage we need to remember that the dark night is "an inflow of God into the soul" (N.2.5.1). Thus, the "active" night comprises what we do, the choices we make that create an opening in our lives through which God can enter.

John calls his counsels "an abridged method" of entering the dark night. In short, John does not provide us with specific behaviors that we should practice. Rather, his counsels are very general in nature and often leave the reader wondering, "So what is he saying we should do?"

The abridged quality of John's counsels makes them susceptible to misinterpretation. Their terseness, in combination with John's stark style and lack of clarifying examples, makes them difficult to interpret. In consequence, the reader must always be on guard, lest he or she project erroneous interpretations upon them.

Furthermore, the reader must appropriate John's counsels to the unique contours of his or her own soul and the concrete circumstances of his or her own life. There is no one correct way or better way to practice John's counsels. The important questions that we need to ask ourselves regarding John's counsels are the following: Is my practice of these counsels helping me to become more attuned to the voice of God? Are they assisting me to grow in charity?

We need to keep in mind that these counsels are means to an end. And the end for which we should all be striving is the fulfillment of the two great commandments: to love God and to love neighbor. With this perspective in mind, let us begin to look at the first counsel.

Counsel One
GROWING IN HABITUAL DESIRE

First, have habitual desire to imitate Christ in all your deeds by bringing your life into conformity with His. You must then study His life in order to know how to imitate Him and behave in all events as He would. (A.1.13.3)

HABITUAL DESIRE

St. Teresa of Avila writes, "Sometimes I think I have great courage and that I wouldn't turn from anything of service to God; and when put to the test, I do have this courage for some things. Another day will come in which I won't find the courage in me to kill even an ant for God if in doing so I'd meet with any opposition" (W.38.6).

In the same vein, St. Thérèse of Lisieux writes that often "in the morning, we feel no courage, no strength to practice virtue" (L.467).

This is the human condition. Our emotional zeal to do God's will waxes and wanes. It rises and falls with the fluctuations of our physical health, mental outlook, and emotional state of soul, much of which is beyond our control. However, in this counsel, John is not talking about our zeal to do God's will; he is talking about our desire.

In Scholastic philosophy, desire is the movement of the will toward the good. Sometimes this movement is accompanied by the affect, or "feeling," of zeal and sometimes it is not. The focus of John's counsel is on doing not on feeling. Thus, we may rephrase John's counsel as follows: "Try to imitate Christ in all that you *do*." The distinction between emotion and desire (as the Scholastics use the term) is crucial in understanding this counsel in particular and the goal of John's spirituality in general. The goal of John's spirituality is union with God through love. It is a union of wills.

In considering this counsel, we must keep in mind the distinction between desire and emotion. As we grow in the spiritual life, our determination to do God's will is strengthened, but this does not mean that our emotions become less vulnerable to the ordinary vicissitudes of daily life. Consider the following incident from the life of St. Teresa.

At midnight, on the eve of the feast of the Assumption, 1567, St. Teresa and her companions entered the city of Medina del Campo to found a new convent. Immediately, they set to work. When dawn arrived, an altar was erected; the Eucharist was celebrated, and the Blessed Sacrament was reserved. Teresa comments:

> Up to this point I was very happy because for me it is the greatest consolation to see one church more where the Blessed Sacrament is preserved. But my happiness did not last long. For when Mass was finished I went to look a little bit through a window at the courtyard, and I saw that all the walls in some places had fallen to the ground and that many days would be required to repair them. Oh, God help me! When I saw His Majesty placed in the street, at a time so dangerous, on account of those Lutherans, what anguish came to my heart. To this anguish were joined all the difficulties that those who had strongly criticized the project

could bring up. I understood clearly that those persons were right. It seemed impossible for me to go ahead with what had been begun. Just as previously everything seemed easy to me when I reflected that I was doing it for God, so now my temptation constricted the Lord's power to such an extent that it didn't seem I had received any favor from Him. Only my lowliness and my powerlessness did I have before me. . . . Also it seemed to me that since this first attempt had gone wrong, everything that I had understood I must do for the Lord in the future would not come about. Then, in addition, came the fear concerning whether or not what I understood in prayer was an illusion. (F.3.10)

While none of us has had Teresa's life experience, many of us can relate to her emotional reaction. Teresa's anxiety, triggered by a small event, causes her to go into a tailspin. Teresa sees a wall that has fallen into ruin, and instantly her imagination runs wild. "The Lutherans will desecrate the Blessed Sacrament!" But there are no Lutherans in Spain; the Inquisition has guaranteed this fact. Even though Teresa is aware of this reality, fearful imaginings run roughshod over her reason. Teresa's anxious mind may have imagined Lutherans launching covert operations in Spain. She had heard stories of Protestants desecrating the Blessed Sacrament in France, and her fears parachuted them over the Pyrenees.

Furthermore, Teresa's anxiety engulfed her in self-doubt. "I should have never undertaken this project. My critics were right. I have deceived myself; the establishment of this convent is not of God's design. I know that from now on everything that I do will fail."

Teresa's overreaction is expressive of two common ways that our mind distorts reality, what cognitive psychologists call "emotional reasoning" and "overgeneralization." Emotional reasoning is the assumption that our negative feelings are a reflection of reality: "I'm afraid that Lutherans will desecrate the Blessed Sacrament; therefore, it must be true." Overgeneralization is seeing a single negative event as the beginning of a never-ending pattern of failure: "It seemed to me that since this *first* attempt had gone wrong, *everything* that I had understood I must do for the Lord in the future would not come about" (F.3.11; italics added). It is important to know that eleven years before this event occurred, Teresa had received the grace of spiritual betrothal. However, even though Teresa had reached this high degree of sanctity, she was still vulnerable to the common anxieties of life.

This event in Teresa's life corrects a common misunderstanding about the nature of holiness. Holiness conforms our will to God's and increases our desire to do his will. It does not eradicate our humanity in the process. There is no contradiction between growing in "habitual desire to imitate Christ in our deeds" and simultaneously feeling extremely anxious or apprehensive.

It is very important to differentiate spiritual growth from emotional healing. The latter sometimes takes place because of the former, but not always. They are not identical. Growing in the process of loving our neighbor does not mean that our feelings toward our neighbor necessarily change. There are certain people in our lives that no matter how much we grow in loving them, we will never like them. And God doesn't expect us to.

Similarly, as we grow spiritually, temptations regarding certain sins may not decrease. Why? Only God knows. Sometimes God allows us to be tempted in order that we can grow in virtue. As St. Thérèse once said, "Keep in mind the method used to make copper objects shine. You smear them with mud after which they will shine like gold. Temptations are like mud for the soul. They serve to make the virtues, which are opposed to these temptations, to shine forth."[16]

Temptations and our lack of emotional zeal to do God's will are not obstacles on the spiritual path. They are blessings in disguise. They make our choices to do God's will more difficult and, in consequence, exact from us a greater degree of charity. And charity is at the heart of John's spirituality. He directs us to grow in habitual desire to imitate Christ in our deeds. All of his counsels are means to one end—union with God through love.

> *For Reflection* Are there strong emotions in my life (e.g., anxiety or anger) that I have always considered obstacles to spiritual growth? Have I ever considered that these "obstacles" are really the contexts through which I can grow in holiness? What temptations in my life are the "mud" for my soul?

THE IMITATION OF CHRIST

"You must then study His life in order to know how to imitate Him and behave in all events as He would" (A.1.13.3). This aspect of the first counsel can also be easily misinterpreted. We have an example of this in the life of Angelo Roncalli, the future Pope John XXIII. In 1903, shortly before making his subdiaconate retreat, Roncalli came to an important insight into the nature of holiness. He wrote:

> Practical experience has now convinced me of this: the concept of holiness which I had formed and applied to myself was mistaken. In every one of my actions, and in the little failings of which I was immediately aware, I used to call to mind the image of some saint whom I had set myself to imitate down to the smallest particular, as a painter makes an exact copy of a picture of Raphael. I used to say to myself: in this case St. Aloysius would have done so and so, or: he would not do this or that. However, it turned out that I was never able to achieve what I had thought I could do, and this worried me. The method was wrong. From the saints I must take the substance, not the [accidentals], of their virtues. I am not St. Aloysius, nor must I seek holiness in his particular way, but according to the requirements of my own nature, my own character, and the different conditions of my life. I must not be the dry, bloodless reproduction of a model, however perfect. God desires us to follow the examples of the saints by absorbing the vital sap of their virtues and turning it into our own life-blood, adapting it to our own individual capacities and particular circumstances. If St. Aloysius had been as I am, he would have become holy in a different way.[17]

Roncalli's youthful zeal mistook a model to be imitated for a mold to be duplicated. This is a common mistake of fledgling souls. In their zeal to "imitate Christ in all of [their] deeds," they are unable to differentiate the "accidents," or accidentals, of a virtue from its substance. Or as St. Teresa of Avila writes in regard to our desire to follow the example of the saints, "We must distinguish what is to be *admired* from what is to be *imitated*" (L.13.4; italics added).

John bids us to "study" (*considerar*) the life of Christ. *Considerar* means to ponder, to consider, to reflect upon. And what we are called to reflect upon is how God is calling us to practice the virtues we see in Christ's life, rather than to replicate Christ's behavior.

St. Francis de Sales teaches that the exercise of virtue must conform to our state in life. He writes, "At the creation God commanded the plants to bear fruit each according to its kind and He likewise commands Christians, the living branches of the vine, to bear fruit by practicing devotion according to their state in life. . . . Is the solitary life of a Carthusian suited to a bishop? Should those who are married practice the poverty of a Capuchin? Should workmen spend as much time in church as a religious? Such devotion would be ridiculous and cause intolerable disorder."[18] The saint's point is clear. Even though solitude, poverty, and prayer (understood as spending time in church) are commendable practices in themselves, they do not exist in themselves, that is, in isolation from the concrete circumstances and responsibilities of our life's calling.

Whenever we are thinking of incorporating an ascetical practice into our life, we need to ascertain whether or not it will be detrimental to fulfilling our obligations in life. Let's take the example of Jake, a construction worker, who has come to believe that God is calling him to fast for the salvation of souls. By all means, Jake should take this call seriously. But what form this fasting will take needs to be discerned.

A common danger at this juncture is imprudence. Let us say that at the time Jake becomes aware that God is calling him to fast, he is reading the life of St. Thumbelina, a fourth-century hermitess who lived in a cave for forty years, fasted every day from sunrise to sunset, and ate tree bark for her evening meal. In his zeal, Jake tries to emulate St. Thumbelina, minus the eating of tree bark. But in a short period of time, Jake realizes that he cannot fast in the same way that St. Thumbelina did. The reason is obvious; Jake's lifestyle is far different from St. Thumbelina's. Jake's job involves strenuous physical labor that requires a high caloric intake. Jake tried to fast like St. Thumbelina, but it didn't work; he became so faint that he couldn't do his job properly. St. Thumbelina's ascetical lifestyle may be appropriate for a ninety-five-pound hermitess living in a cave, but not for a two-hundred-pound construction worker operating a jackhammer from dawn to dusk. John Cassian, expressing the prudent wisdom of the desert, writes, "And so on the manner of fasting a uniform rule cannot easily be observed, because everybody does not have the same strength . . . fasting has to do with the possibilities of the body."[19]

St. John of the Cross tells us that our ascetical practices should be performed with "order and discretion" (A.1.13.7). And as St. Thomas Aquinas writes in his *Summa Theologica*,[20] discretion or prudence is "right reason applied to human conduct." It is the ability to discern and distinguish what is appropriate for every situation. It is perfected practical reason, the art of making right decisions in the light of objective reality.

It was not prudent for Jake to try to fast like St. Thumbelina because it was unrealistic. A devotion or ascetical practice should never conflict with the responsibilities and obligations of our life. All of us are called to practice the virtues that we see in the life of Christ. However, we need to practice them according to our station in life. When John writes that we should "imitate [Christ] and behave in all events as He would," John is not advocating a mindless process of spiritual cloning. He is exhorting us to make Christ a model to be imitated, rather than a mold to be duplicated.

For Reflection	Is there a specific virtue that God is calling me to focus on at this time in my life? How do I believe God is asking me to practice this virtue?

INFORMING THE MIND AND NOURISHING THE SPIRIT

John tells us that the first step in knowing how to imitate Christ is to study his life. "You must then study His life in order to know how to imitate Him and behave in all events as He would" (A.1.13.3). This counsel "to study" (*considerar*: to ponder, to consider, or to reflect upon) the life of Christ is meant to be not merely an intellectual exercise but also a meditative process that simultaneously informs the mind and nourishes the spirit. The classical practice of prayerful reading of the Scriptures called *lectio divina*, or "divine reading," comes closest to what John means by *considerar*.

The question now arises, what should be the subject matter of our considerations? What should our diet of spiritual reading consist of? Obviously the Scriptures, especially the New Testament, should be our common fare. However, we should be careful of interpreting John's counsel too narrowly. Our selection of spiritual reading should be guided by its overall purpose, namely, to nourish our minds and to dispose our hearts to do the will of God. In light of this goal, we should not restrict our spiritual reading to texts that are either explicitly Christian or even spiritual in nature. There are two fundamental reasons this is important.

First, sometimes the instrument that God uses to awaken our hearts will be a secular or even a pagan text. We have an example of this in the life of St. Augustine. When Augustine was a young student of rhetoric, he read Cicero's exhortation to philosophy, titled *Hortensius*. It was a book that changed his life. Augustine wrote, "The book changed my way of feeling and the character of my prayers to You, O Lord, for under its influence my petitions and desires altered. All my hollow hopes suddenly seemed worthless, and with unbelievable intensity my heart burned with longing for the immortality that wisdom seemed to promise. I began to rise up in order to return to You."[21] Conversely, when Augustine read the Bible at this time in his life, it did not touch his heart. In fact, he was repulsed by its unpolished style, as compared to the authors of classical antiquity. This chapter in Augustine's life is an example of a principle by which God guides the soul. John tells us that God guides the soul gently, with order and *according to the mode of the receiver* (see A.2.17.2; italics added). Augustine did not have the capacity to perceive the wisdom of the Scriptures as a student of rhetoric because of the great value he placed on the style of a text. Thus, the instrument that God used to awaken desire in Augustine's heart had to correspond to the person Augustine was at this time in his life, rather than to the person he would become.

The second reason we should not restrict our spiritual reading to explicitly spiritual books follows upon the first. Just as God leads us according to our nature, so too, we should respect the unique contours of our own soul. What nourishes my soul may not nourish your soul.

When I conduct retreats, a discussion frequently arises regarding spiritual reading. At times, I have received strange looks when I share with the group that one of my favorite "spiritual" authors is Charles Dickens. I tell the group that I cannot explain why I am so touched by Dickens's works. All I know is that his writings nourish my vision; they help me to look upon people with compassion. Nevertheless, I would never recommend that everyone read Dickens, for the criterion that should govern the authors we ingest is the effect that their works have upon us. Do they help to fulfill the purpose of John's first counsel, namely, do they help to enkindle our desire to imitate Christ? Do they help sustain the movement of the will toward the good? Do they foster growth in virtue and provide encouragement and support in time of temptation? Authors that nourish your soul in such ways should be your companions on life's journey.

For Reflection	What specific authors or works nourish my soul?

Counsel Two
Renouncing Sensory Satisfaction

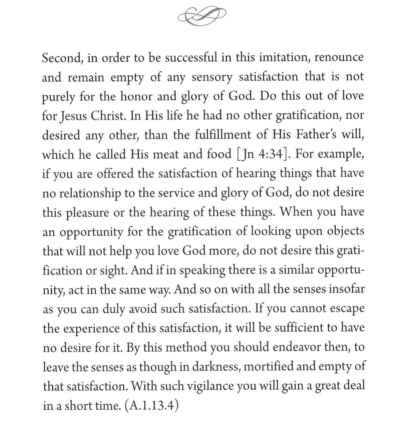

Second, in order to be successful in this imitation, renounce and remain empty of any sensory satisfaction that is not purely for the honor and glory of God. Do this out of love for Jesus Christ. In His life he had no other gratification, nor desired any other, than the fulfillment of His Father's will, which he called His meat and food [Jn 4:34]. For example, if you are offered the satisfaction of hearing things that have no relationship to the service and glory of God, do not desire this pleasure or the hearing of these things. When you have an opportunity for the gratification of looking upon objects that will not help you love God more, do not desire this gratification or sight. And if in speaking there is a similar opportunity, act in the same way. And so on with all the senses insofar as you can duly avoid such satisfaction. If you cannot escape the experience of this satisfaction, it will be sufficient to have no desire for it. By this method you should endeavor then, to leave the senses as though in darkness, mortified and empty of that satisfaction. With such vigilance you will gain a great deal in a short time. (A.1.13.4)

This counsel sounds uncomplicated. If you want to imitate Christ, mortify your sensual appetites. Yes, this is the counsel's core message. However, since the counsel's meaning can be easily misinterpreted, it is important for us to explore what the counsel is *not* saying. John is not condemning all sensual pleasure. The mere fact that he says we should "renounce and remain empty of every sensory satisfaction that is not purely for the honor and glory of God" implies that there are pleasures that give God honor and glory. For example, all of us need healthy forms of relaxation that foster our physical, emotional, and spiritual well-being. Cassian relates the following story about John the Evangelist.

> It is said that the blessed John, while he was gently stroking a partridge with his hands, suddenly saw a philosopher approaching him in the garb of a hunter, who was astonished that a man of so great fame and reputation should demean himself to such paltry and trivial amusements, and said: "Can you be that John, whose great and famous reputation attracted me with the greatest desire for your acquaintance? Why then do you occupy yourself with such poor amusements?" John responded, "That bow you are carrying in your hand, do you always carry it bent?" "No" replied the philosopher, "for the force of its stiffness needs to be relaxed because if it were continually bent, the bow would be lessened and destroyed . . . its stiffness would be lost by excessive and continuous strain, and it would be impossible for the more powerful arrows to be shot." "And my lad," said the blessed John, "do not let this slight and short relaxation of my mind disturb you, as unless it sometimes relieved and relaxed the rigor of its purpose by some recreation, the spirit would lose its spring owing to the unbroken strain, and would be unable when need required, implicitly to follow what was right."[22]

St. Francis de Sales, commenting upon this story, writes, "It is certainly wrong to be so strict with oneself, so austere and unsociable, as to deny oneself and *everyone else*, recreation" (italics added).[23] In this regard, St. Thomas asks the question, "Can there be sin in a lack of play?" His answer is an emphatic "Yes!" He argues that a lack of play and recreation is not only intemperate but also uncharitable, for when we deprive ourselves of necessary pleasure, we become morose and burdensome to others—in other words, a wet blanket on others' enjoyment.[24]

Usually we associate sin and inordinate sensual pleasure with excess. However, St. Thomas reminds us that pleasure can be inordinate by deficiency as well as excess, for temperance that regulates our use of pleasure, like every virtue, is a mean between two extremes. We can be intemperate regarding pleasure by deficiency as much as by excess. Sensory pleasure is important in the spiritual life. St. Thomas teaches that this is especially imperative for those "occupied in the works of contemplation" for the pleasures derived through the senses refresh the fatigued mind and spirit.[25]

John's counsel regarding the mortification of sensory pleasure is austere, but St. Thomas reminds us, "Austerity as a virtue does not banish all pleasures, but such only as are excessive and inordinate."[26] The wisdom of these words is rooted in the common experience that one extreme leads to another. If austerity is too austere, it creates the very thing it tries to avoid: self-indulgence. John Cassian writes, "We must seek in all humility to acquire the grace of discernment which can keep us safe from the two kinds of excess. For there is an old saying: 'Excesses meet.' Too much fasting and too much eating come to the same end. . . . Too much self-denial brings weakness and induces the same condition of carelessness. Often I have seen men who could not be snared by gluttony fall, nevertheless, through immoderate fasting and tumble in weakness into the very urge which they had overcome."[27] In the same vein, "Aristotle wisely observed that human beings cannot live without pleasure. Pleasure is a real good that satisfies one of man's basic needs . . . and if human beings are deprived of the pleasures of the spirit, they are likely to indulge inordinately in the pleasures of the flesh."[28] As stated earlier, the enemy is not pleasure per se but inordinate pleasure.

So far we have explored what this counsel does not say. John is not advocating a morose spirituality that drains life of joy and pleasure. Nevertheless, John is cognizant of the fact that our relationship to pleasures, even legitimate ones, needs to be controlled and that the choices we exercise in the area of pleasure are important for our spiritual welfare. Just as we can misinterpret John as advocating the elimination of all sensual pleasure from our lives, so too, can we conveniently skip over his teaching that it is necessary to deprive ourselves of sensual pleasures in order to enter into the dark night (A.1.3.1). John's teaching on ascetical practices is neither Manichean nor Epicurean; he is neither rigorous nor lax. He is realistic.

John's teaching is based upon the reality that there are certain objects, persons, substances, situations, and so on, that we have to either modify our use of or keep a distance from, not because they are bad in themselves, but because we don't have the capacity to use them without suffering spiritual damage. All of us have our fatal attractions. We need to keep our distance from certain objects, not because they are evil but because we lack the capacity to use them without abusing them. There are certain objects that we cannot possess without becoming possessed by them.

One of the central themes in J. R. R. Tolkien's trilogy *The Lord of the Rings* is the inability to wield absolute power (symbolized by the One Ring) without becoming possessed by it. This is why the truly wise characters in the story, Elrond,

Gandalf, and Galadriel, refuse to accept the Ring when it is offered to them. Their wisdom is rooted in humble self-knowledge. They know that even though their intentions may be pure, their wills are weak and flawed. An essential part of wisdom is knowing what we cannot handle.

All of us are vulnerable to becoming addicted or inordinately attached to certain experiences that gratify either our senses or our ego. For John, the nature of the object is secondary to our relationship to it; for even good things and healthy activities can prove to be obstacles to spiritual growth if our relationship to them becomes inordinate. For example, reading a book on the spirituality of St. John of the Cross is not intrinsically evil. Nevertheless, such an activity can become an obstacle to doing God's will. For example, people can become so absorbed in reading John that they neglect the demands of charity and are remiss in performing daily duties. We can be nourished or devoured by books. It all depends on our relationship to them. It is not enough to ask whether an activity is objectively good or bad. We also need to discern whether our relationship to an activity is advantageous or detrimental to our spiritual growth.

For example, St. Thérèse loved to read so much that she once said she could have spent her whole life reading. However, because she knew the danger of becoming absorbed in books, she chose "not to go beyond a certain time in [her] reading" (S.71). Reading per se was not the issue. In fact, Thérèse said that certain books proved to be some of "the greatest graces in [her] life" (S.102).

Imposing limits upon gratifying our desires does not restrict our lives. Rather, it frees us from becoming self-absorbed. And the less we are preoccupied with an earthly pursuit, the more we are capable of being consciously aware of God's presence.

For Reflection

Is my relationship to sensual pleasures intemperate by either excess or deficiency? In this regard, what do I need to do in order to have a healthy relationship to the pleasures of the senses?

ENDEAVOR TO BE INCLINED . . .

Many blessings flow when the four natural passions (joy, hope, fear, and sorrow) are in harmony and at peace. The following maxims contain a complete method for mortifying and quieting them. If put into practice, these maxims will give rise to abundant merit and great virtues.

> Endeavor to be inclined always:
> not to the easiest, but to the most difficult;
> not to the most delightful, but to the most distasteful;
> not to the most gratifying, but to the less pleasant;
> not to what means rest for you, but to hard work;
> not to the consoling, but to the unconsoling;
> not to the most, but to the least;
> not to the highest and most precious, but to the lowest and most despised;
> not to wanting something, but to wanting nothing.
> Do not go about looking for the best of temporal things, but for the worst,
> and, for Christ, desire to enter into complete nakedness, emptiness,
> and poverty in everything in the world.

You should embrace these practices earnestly and try to overcome the repugnance of your will toward them. If you sincerely put them into practice with order and discretion, you will discover in them great delight and consolation. (A.1.13.6–7).

As we approach this counsel, we should be clear about what it does *not* say. John does not say that we should always *do* that which is most difficult. Rather, he states that we should endeavor to be inclined (*inclinarse*) to the most difficult. John is referring to developing a habit of mind that inclines our will toward the practice of virtue. There are many means by which we can develop and sustain this habit of mind. Let us consider a simple example:

It's Friday morning and I'm working at my desk. I'm also on door and phone duty, a task I need to brace myself for because I have no patience with and less sympathy for telemarketers. It is necessary for me to exert effort merely to speak to them in a civil tone of voice. In consequence, when I am caught off guard or in a foul mood, I have, on occasion, been downright rude.

I have found two practices that have helped me guard against rudeness and incline my will toward patience. The first is to let the phone ring three times before lifting the receiver. This provides me with a moment to make an act of the will to be kind and patient to the caller. Second, I have taped on the front of my computer a copy of an illustration of Mr. Neckett, a character from Dickens's novel *Bleak House*.

Neckett is a bailiff's man. His job is to arrest debtors and throw them into prison. Because of his office, he is despised. Neckett also hates his work but has a sick wife and three children to care for, and this is the only employment available to him. What choice does he have?

When I reflect upon Neckett's situation, I feel a sense of compassion for him. This has led me to consider that maybe the telemarketers whom I find so annoying may be like Neckett. They may be trapped in a job by their life circumstances, a job that subjects them to rude treatment.

Having Neckett's image on my computer helps to foster a feeling of sympathy and keeps a choice before me. I can be patient or rude. Neckett's image is an aid that inclines my will toward the loving deed. But this inclination can only survive if I act upon it. We lose patience because we don't practice it.

For *Reflection*

What means could I employ to incline my will to practice virtue? How can I use these means effectively?

ENDEAVOR TO BE INCLINED (*CONTINUED*)

What John is contrasting in his series of counsels are two basic orientations of the will that result in two fundamentally different lifestyles. The first is a life that seeks the path of least resistance and is inclined to the easiest, the most delightful, and the most gratifying. It tries to eliminate every form of exertion, attempts to find the easy way out of every situation, and goes to lengths to avoid every inconvenience.

At first glance, we might think that a person who lives such a life would be happy and at peace. However, John would say that even though such a lifestyle provides moments of relief from the hassle and inconveniences of daily life, in the long run it would make the person miserable. But how can seeking the most delightful, the easiest, and so forth, cause misery? John would argue as follows. The more our goal in life is to seek the easy way out of every situation, to do the minimum in every allotted task, to cut corners in every duty, to dodge every request, and to avoid every inconvenience and discomfort, the more burdensome life becomes. This is because the more our will is inclined toward the path of least resistance, the more we resist the ordinary demands and requests of daily life. In consequence, we experience life as a grand imposition and intrusion. Every task becomes oppressive, and every request is an egregious tax upon our time and energy. For when our will is inclined toward the easiest, the most delightful, and so on, our desire is forever being frustrated. We become guarded and anxious, lest something intrude upon our settled existence, and we blow up when something does intrude. As psychologist Albert Ellis writes, "The easy way out usually comes off as just that—the easy way out of the most rewarding *life* . . . [and] by avoiding certain difficulties of life, [we] almost always tend to exaggerate their pain and discomfort."[29] In short, we create the misery we try to avoid.

The second orientation of the will results in a lifestyle of self-sacrifice that seeks the will of God and the good of one's neighbor. Here, John makes a paradoxical claim. He says that the more that our will is inclined toward the most difficult, less pleasant, and so forth, the more we will discover "great delight and consolation" (A.1.13.7). But how is such a thing possible? How can doing that which is difficult be consoling? John's response is twofold.

First, he would point out that delight and consolation are fruits of embracing these practices; they are not their immediate effects. They emerge only over a period of time; they are not experienced from the outset. In fact, when a person first begins to practice John's counsels, he or she experiences resistance in the form of repugnance: "Try to overcome the repugnance of your will toward them" (A.1.13.7).

Second, John would point out that the delight and consolation derived from doing God's will is of a nature beyond human calculation. It is a spiritual joy that is an experience of God's presence. For when we choose to do God's will, we become more intimately united to God. The delight and consolation is often not accompanied by emotional elation, but it is a quiet joy that comes from knowing that one is doing the right thing. I believe that this is what John meant when he wrote that "in His life [Jesus] had no other gratification, nor desired any other, than the fulfillment of His Father's will, which he called His meat and food [Jn 4:34]" (A.1.13.4). It is a joy that nourishes the heart.

Finally, it is worth noting how John says that these counsels should be practiced: "with order (*ordenada*) and discretion (*discretamente*)." We may surmise his meaning by what we know of John's life and his writings. John was a very prudent spiritual director who often steered his directees away from the shoals of excessive bodily penances. For example, in his treatment of the faults of "beginners," John writes, "[Some people in their practice of penances] pass beyond the mean in which virtue resides and is acquired. . . . They try to hide these penances from the one whom they owe obedience in such matters. Some even dare perform these penances contrary to obedience. Such individuals are unreasonable. . . . They subordinate submissiveness and obedience . . . to corporeal penance. But corporeal penance without obedience is no more than a penance of beasts" (N.1.6.1–2).

This passage is very instructive regarding what John means by *ordenada* and *discretamente*. One of the meanings of *ordenada* is to direct something to an end. And the end or purpose to which our ascetical practices should be directed is growth in virtue, as understood as a *via media*, the golden mean that avoids both excess and defect. John's allusion to the time-honored Scholastic definition of virtue, coupled with his insistence that a person should not engage in penance without either permission or consultation, points to what John means by *discretamente*. John is saying that there is a lack of judgment, prudence, and discretion if we engage in ascetical practices without being in dialogue with both the wisdom of the tradition of the church and the consultation of the community. As a proverb of the desert tradition has it, "He who has chosen himself as a spiritual guide has chosen a fool."

For Reflection Where in my life is my will inclined toward the path of least resistance? What have been the consequences of giving in to this inclination? When have I experienced the spiritual joy of God's presence as a result of inclining my will to his?

Counsel Three
HAVING CONTEMPT FOR SELF

These counsels if truly carried out are sufficient for entry into the night of sense. But to ensure that we give abundant enough counsel, here is another exercise that teaches mortification of concupiscence of the flesh, concupiscence of the eyes, and pride of life, which, as St. John says, reign in the world and give rise to all the other appetites [1 Jn 2:16]. First, try to act with contempt for yourself and desire that all others do likewise. Second, endeavor to speak in contempt of yourself and desire all others to do so. Third, try to think lowly and contemptuously of yourself and desire that all others do the same. (A.1.13.8–9)

These counsels are without a doubt the most difficult to understand and potentially the most dangerous if misinterpreted. Taken literally, they seem to be advocating masochism. However, we will not find any justification for this interpretation in either John's life or his doctrine.

To correctly understand these counsels, we need to interpret them in the light of their purpose. They are meant to be the means of entering the dark night. Therefore, the contempt that John is advocating is not directed toward ourselves as creatures of immense value and dignity made in God's image and likeness; rather, these counsels are meant to be means to mortify our inordinate appetites that feed our egotistical self.

This interpretation is based on John's reference to the threefold concupiscence (of the flesh, the eyes, and the pride of life), which in the literature of John's day differentiated disordered love from well-ordered love.

In discussing the threefold concupiscence, St. Thomas, summarizing St. Augustine's thought,[30] writes "that inordinate self-love is the cause of all sin [and that] a *properly directed love* of self is both obligatory and natural, so that a man might will for himself those things which are good for him. St. Augustine speaks of *inordinate self love*, which leads to contempt for God"[31]

This distinction between disordered and well-ordered self-love is crucial for a correct understanding of John's counsel. Self-love is not synonymous with selfishness. Well-ordered self-love makes choices that are in our best interest, choices that are aligned with God's will. Disordered self-love is self-destructive.

Restraint is the essence of John's counsel on having contempt for our self-centered thoughts, words, and deeds. Do not allow them access into your life. Do not act upon them. Resist these tendencies toward self-centeredness when they appear at the threshold of consciousness.

For *Reflection*	In what ways do my thoughts, words, or actions feed my egotistical self?

Counsel Four
TO HAVE ALL, RENOUNCE ALL

As a conclusion to these counsels and rules it would be appropriate to repeat the verses in *The Ascent of the Mount* . . . which are instructions for climbing to the summit, the high state of union.

To reach satisfaction in all
desire satisfaction in nothing.
To come to possess all
desire the possession of nothing.
To arrive at being all
desire to be nothing.
To come to the knowledge of all
desire the knowledge of nothing.

To come to enjoy what you have not
you must go by a way in which you enjoy not.
To come to the knowledge you have not
you must go by a way in which you know not.
To come to the possession you have not
you must go by a way in which you possess not.
To come to be what you are not
you must go by a way in which you are not. (A.1.13.10–11)

"He who binds to himself a joy doth the winged life destroy but he who kisses the joy as it flies lives in Eternity's sun rise." The image that comes to my mind when I read these words of William Blake is that of a butterfly that has lighted upon the palm of a woman's hand. As the woman looks at this beautiful creature of God, she is filled with the joy that beauty affords. If she is attached to this aesthetic experience, her joy will be tainted by the anxiety of knowing that it will not last; for the butterfly will eventually fly away. And when it attempts to do so, the woman's possessiveness will clutch at the butterfly and destroy the object of her joy.

Conversely, if the woman is not possessive, she can thoroughly enjoy the butterfly's beauty, for she has the capacity to accept the experience for what it is, a fleeting moment, a transitory gift to give thanks for. We see the consequences of these two stances toward creation reflected in the following passage from *The Ascent*:

> [People] obtain more joy and recreation *in creatures* through the dispossession of them. They cannot rejoice in them if they *behold them with possessiveness*, for this is a care that, like a trap, holds the spirit to the earth and does not allow wideness of heart. In detachment from things they acquire a clearer knowledge of them and a better understanding of both natural and supernatural truths concerning them. . . . They delight in these goods according to the truth of them. . . . Purged of the clouds and appearances of the accidents, [these souls] penetrate the truth and value of things. . . . Those, then, whose joy is unpossessive of things rejoice in them all *as though* they possessed them all; those others, beholding them with a possessive mind, *lose all the delight of them* all

in general. The former . . . though they have nothing, possess everything with greater liberty; the others, insofar as they possess things with attachment, neither have nor possess anything. Rather, their heart is held by things and they suffer as a captive. As many as are the joys they long to uncover in creatures, so many will necessarily be the straits and afflictions of their attached and possessed heart. (A.3.20.2–3; italics added)

The word *anxiety*, derived from the Latin *angustus*, meaning narrow or to choke, is very descriptive of what we feel when we are anxious. We feel hemmed in because anxiety causes an involuntary tightening of the chest and neck, which constricts our breathing and causes a feeling of being choked.

Anxiety, says John, is one of the symptoms of possessiveness. He compares it to a trap. The Spanish word that John uses for trap is *lazo*, which is a lariat, a noose, or a slipknot used to snare animals. That is, possessiveness is a rope that tightens around its prey, makes it feel trapped, and engenders anxiety. Anxiety breeds anxiety. The more possessive people feel anxious, the more they clutch their possessions, and this makes them more anxious. This phenomenon is illustrated by the following story:

Once there was an avaricious king who had a nightmare. The king consulted his wizard regarding the meaning of his dream. The wizard said that the dream was an evil apparition that predicted that on the king's birthday an enemy would plunder his possessions. Out of fear, the king ordered that all of his riches be placed in his throne room and surrounded by a hundred of his most trusted guards. As his birthday approached, the king became more anxious. This anxiety made him so suspicious of some of his guards that he had them killed. Then the king moved his riches to a smaller room that had only one entrance and posted fifty guards at the door. On the eve of his birthday, the king's anxiety reached a level of panic when he noticed that there was a small window in the room through which an enemy might enter. So an hour before midnight, he ordered that his possessions be transferred again, this time to a cramped, windowless dungeon cell. The king entered the cell and ordered that the entranceway be bricked up and torn down the day after his birthday. His orders were carried out. The day after the king's birthday, the king's men broke down the wall and found their sovereign dead—he had suffocated.

This king's death brought the truth to light. He had never possessed anything; rather, he had become possessed by what he had. The story is an illustration of John's words, that a possessive "heart is *held* by things and [it] suffers as a *captive*" (A.3.20.3; italics added).

Conversely, John teaches that it is only the nonpossessive heart that is truly free, and although such persons "have nothing, possess everything with greater liberty" (A.3.20.3). This paradoxical truth was expressed by St. Thérèse when one of her novices confessed that she was envious of Thérèse's gifts and talents. Thérèse responded, "If I love the good that is in my neighbor as much as he loves it himself, that good is as much mine as it is his."[32] In short, nonpossessiveness releases us from the trap of envy and frees us to rejoice in all things. This is the goal of John's admonitions: to grow in our capacity to find satisfaction in all things, even to the extent that we can "come to enjoy what [we] *have not*" (A.1.13.11; italics added).

For
Reflection

Is possessiveness holding me captive? What are the effects of this possessiveness (e.g., anxiety, envy, etc.)? What do I believe I need to do to free myself from the trap of possessiveness so that I can find satisfaction in all things?

The Fatal Pause

When you delay in something
you cease to rush toward the all.
For to go from the all to the all
you must deny yourself of all in all.
And when you come to the possession of the all
you must possess it without wanting anything.
Because if you desire to have something in all
your treasure in God is not purely your all. (A.1.13.12)

Flannery O'Connor writes that "there is a moment in every great story in which the presence of grace can be felt as it waits to be accepted or rejected."[33] We have an example of this in Anton Chekhov's story "At the Mill." The story is about a rich miller named Alexey Birukov. One day, Alexey's mother comes to visit her son at the mill. Her purpose is to beg Alexey for some money for his brother Vasily, who is wretchedly poor and is unable to provide for his family. "'I have come to beg you for help. . . . After all he is your brother. . . . He is poor but you are rich; you have a mill of your own, and orchards, and you trade in fish. The Lord has given you intelligence and bounty—and you are all alone. But Vasily has four children, and I the accursed one, am a burden to him, and all he earns is seven rubles. How can he feed us all on that?' In silence the miller carefully filled his pipe."[34] After a time,

Alexey responds, "It isn't your business to meddle in other people's affairs." Realizing that her entreaties have fallen on deaf ears, Alexey's mother decides to leave. But before doing so, she takes a small spice cake out of a bundle and gives it to Alexey. "Yesterday I was at the deaconess's house and they passed something around. So I put one away for you." Alexey is angry and tells his mother to leave and pushes her hand away. The spice cake falls to the ground. As Alexey's mother walks away,

> An emotion long dormant stirred within his breast, something like an expression of fear flashed across his face. "Maminka!" he called. The old woman started and looked back. The miller hurriedly plunged his hand into his pocket and drew out a large leather purse. "There," he mumbled, pulling out of the purse a wad of paper money in which some silver coins were stuck, "take it!" He rolled the wad in his hand, crushed it . . . then fingered it again. The bills and the silver coins, slipping between his fingers, dropped back into the purse one after another, and only a twenty-kopeck piece remained in his hand. The miller examined it, rubbed it between his fingers and, groaning and getting purple, handed it to his mother.[35]

The money that slipped back into Alexey's purse is symbolic of the dormant compassion that had been awakened within him but had sunk back into his heart. The story could have had a different ending if Alexey had not paused and rubbed his money between his fingers. That was the fatal moment. It provided enough space for greed to defeat his better impulses. Something died within Alexy at that moment: "*groaning and getting purple*, he handed [the twenty-kopeck piece] to his mother." The moment passed; an opportunity slipped by.

Literally, it had slipped through his fingers. Life is a series of fleeting moments, crossroads of choice at which we must choose either to respond to God's inspirations to love or to turn a deaf ear to them.

In the above counsel, John focuses on the crossroads that we see in Chekhov's story, those moments between inspiration and choice. John warns us to be on guard when we hesitate in our response to doing God's will. "When you delay (*reparas*) in something you cease to rush (*arrojarte*) toward the all" (A.1.13.12). *Reparas* means to delay in order to consider or reflect upon. *Arrojarte*, when translated metaphorically, means to respond with a certain abandon.

In the space of a pause, our fears, our selfishness, and our laziness can talk us out of a decision. In his counsel, John is not advocating making reckless life decisions. Rather, he is cautioning us not to linger at the daily crossroads of life, when we encounter the ordinary demands of charity. For in those moments of hesitation, like Alexey, we can talk ourselves out of what we know God is asking us to do.

For Reflection	What are the daily situations in which I am confronted with the choice of either holding on to or parting with the "coinage" of my time and energy? What factors tend to make me stingy in this regard? Can I recall moments of hesitation when I talked myself out of doing what I knew God was asking me to do?

The Sweet Breast of God

A love of pleasure, and attachment to it, usually fires the will toward the enjoyment of things that give pleasure. A more intense enkindling of another, better love (love of the soul's Bridegroom) is necessary for the vanquishing of the appetites and the denial of this pleasure. By finding satisfaction and strength in this love, it will have the courage and constancy to readily deny all other appetites. (A.1.14.2)

In a previous reflection, "Coming to Terms," I pointed out that God uses the pleasure of divine consolation to wean a soul away from overly indulging in earthly pleasures. In this reflection, we will consider how this divine consolation is experienced by the soul.

In the above passage, John says that the grace of consolation is experienced as an enkindling of desire for God. However, at the beginning of *The Dark Night*, John states that the grace of consolation is experienced as a cessation of temptation. "The soul states that it was able to make this escape because of the strength and warmth gained from loving its Bridegroom in this contemplation . . . for that night of purifying contemplation lulled to sleep and deadened all the inordinate movements of the passions and appetites in the house of sense" (N. Explanation. 2). Perhaps, what John is describing are two forms of the same grace. Sometimes the grace is experienced as enthusiasm and energy that draws us toward God: "fired with love's urgent longings." At other times, the grace enables a soul to walk away from worldly attachments because they cease to have a hold upon it: "my house now being all stilled." (See the poem "The Dark Night," stanza 1, in the *Ascent*.)

The essence of the grace is what it accomplishes rather than how the grace is experienced. Whether divine consolation enkindles desire that enables a soul to embrace a new life or whether it lulls to sleep the soul's inordinate appetites that allow it to walk away from its old life, the effect is the same.

Why consolation is experienced in different ways, no one knows. Perhaps it is due to personal differences. Some people tend to be naturally energetic, enthusiastic, and high spirited, whereas others tend to be more reserved and reflective and not given to exuberance. If God, as John contends, leads the soul "according to the mode of the receiver," then it would stand to reason that God's grace respects our individuality.

For Reflection

John tells us that God leads us according to the mode of the receiver; that is, God's grace is in conformity with the type of person we are. In what ways do I experience the consolation of God—through peace, joy, courage, or enthusiasm?

BOOK
TWO

The Withdrawal of Consolation

Toward the end of book one of *The Ascent*, John tells us that God lures a soul away from its former way of life by means of consolation, which renders prayer enjoyable and the practice of virtue effortless. However, there comes a time when God withdraws the sweet breast of consolation. In the light of this experience, many people wonder, "What is the relationship between consolation and the spiritual life?" John seems to anticipate this question in the opening chapter of book two of *The Ascent*. He writes, "To enter the night of sense and denude itself of sensible things, the soul needed the longings of sensitive love. But all that is required for complete pacification of the spiritual house is the negation through pure faith of all the spiritual faculties and gratifications and appetites. This achieved, the soul will be joined with the Beloved in union of simplicity and purity and love and likeness" (A.2.1.2).

There is a twofold spiritual truth contained in this passage. First, consolation, the felt sense of God's presence, or what John calls here "the longings of sensitive love," is not necessary for spiritual growth. Second, John even implies that the absence of consolation is the condition in which we grow in solid virtue. By way of analogy, we all know that it takes more effort to be patient with people when we have a cold or are fatigued than when we are feeling well. Similarly, it is more virtuous to do God's will when we do not have the emotional support of consolation.

We need to understand that the lack of consolation is an indication not that God is absent but rather that he is present in a different way. In consolation, the soul experiences God in the effortlessness to practice virtue; however, when consolation is withdrawn, the soul experiences God in the strength to struggle against temptation.

For *Reflection*	When I am struggling against temptation without experiencing God's consoling presence, have I ever thought that he is supporting me with his strengthening presence?

The Passive Night of Sense

When a person is a beginner in the life of prayer, one of the things that happens when God withdraws consolation is that the individual is no longer able to draw sweetness from meditations or find solace in the practice of virtue. The golden glow of God's presence has evaporated; the relish of all things spiritual has vanished; everything is dry.

This withdrawal of sensible consolation results in a twofold crisis that John calls the passive night of sense. First, it is a crisis of choice. Will the soul continue to pray and practice virtue without the support of consolation, or will it give up? Second, it is a crisis of confusion. This is because many beginners have the erroneous belief that the barometer that gauges God's presence in their lives is the intensity of consolation that they experience. Therefore, when consolation is absent, they think that God has withdrawn from them, and they do not know why.

In *The Screwtape Letters*, C. S. Lewis writes of God's loving design at the heart of this twofold crisis. Lewis's work is in the form of a series of letters from Screwtape, an undersecretary to the High Command of Hell, to his nephew Wormwood, a junior tempter, who has been assigned to a young male "patient." Screwtape offers the following perspective to Wormwood, who is overjoyed that his patient, who has recently been converted to Christianity, has lost his zeal for things spiritual.

The Enemy [God] allows this disappointment to occur on the threshold of every human endeavor. . . . Desiring their freedom, He therefore refuses to carry them, by their mere affections and habits, to any of the goals which He sets before them: He leaves them to "do it on their own." And there lies our opportunity. But also, remember, there lies our danger. If once they get through their initial dryness successfully, they become much less dependent on emotion and therefore much harder to tempt. . . . You must have often wondered why the Enemy does not make more use of His power to be sensibly present to human souls in any degree He chooses and at any moment. But the Irresistible and the Indisputable are the two weapons which the very nature of His scheme forbids Him to use. Merely to over-ride a human will (as His felt presence in any but the faintest and most mitigated degree would certainly do) would be for Him useless. He cannot ravish. He can only woo. . . . He is prepared to do a little overriding at the beginning. He will set them off with communications of His presence, which, though faint, seem great to them, with emotional sweetness, and easy conquest over temptation. But He never allows this state of affairs to last long. Sooner or later He withdraws, if not in fact, at least from their conscious experience, all those supports and incentives. He leaves the creature to stand up on its own legs—to carry out from the will alone duties which have lost all relish. It is during such trough periods, much more than during the peak periods, that it is growing into the sort of creature He wants it to be. Hence the prayers offered in the state of dryness are those which please Him best. . . . He cannot "tempt" to virtue as we do to vice. He wants them to learn to walk and must therefore take away His hand; and if only the will to walk is

really there He is pleased even with their stumbles. Do not
be deceived, Wormwood. Our cause is never more in danger
than when a human, no longer desiring, but still intending,
to do our Enemy's will, looks around upon a universe from
which every trace of Him seems to have vanished, and asks
why he has been forsaken, and still obeys.[1]

This passage discloses God's loving design that is at the heart
of the passive night of sense. God wants the best for us; God
wants us to share his divine life, which is love. And this can
only be accomplished with our free consent. This is why God's
consoling presence has to be withdrawn. If we are overpow-
ered by the "Irresistible," our free will is overridden. The soul
must now walk on its own two feet. If it is to advance, it must
choose to continue to be faithful in doing God's will, without
the emotional support of consolation.

The passive night of sense is the beginning of the long
haul. It marks the transition from childhood to adulthood in
the spiritual life. It is the acceptance to struggle to be faithful
in the obligations of life, to be constant in prayer and charity,
regardless of one's moods. It is keeping an even keel in a storm
of anger and frustration and continuing to ply the oar amid
the doldrums and tediousness of routine.

The second major issue is confusion. Like Wormwood's
"patient," the soul going through the passive night of sense
feels that every trace of God has vanished, and it does not
know why. The source of the confusion is the misinterpretation of experience. Beginners believe that there is a direct relationship between the intensity of consolation and both their
holiness and their intimacy with God. Therefore, when consolation evaporates, confusion ensues. They believe that God has
withdrawn and that they are backsliding on the spiritual path.

Or as John puts it, "This change is a surprise to them because everything seems to be functioning in reverse" (N.1.8.3).

These souls believe that they are regressing because they judge their spiritual progress by their feelings. They become confused and frightened, for they can find no explanation for the change. They have been steadfast in their spiritual disciplines and remained constant in the practice of virtue. Yet, the wells of spiritual consolation have dried up.

In such moments of darkness and confusion, John's guidance is a beacon of light. He teaches us not to judge spiritual progress with either an emotional or a psychological yardstick. He reminds us that to go forward on the spiritual path is to do the will of God, irrespective of how we are feeling.

Even though the aspect of the passive night of sense that John focuses on is the transition from discursive meditation to the beginnings of contemplative prayer, we need to keep in mind that the passive night of sense involves every aspect of life. A common analogy for the passive night of sense is the period in a marriage when the honeymoon wanes and the couple begins to grow together in love by means of the daily, unglamorous sacrifices that marriage exacts. This analogy is apt because the type of mortification that is most germane to the passive night of sense is persevering in prayer and the practice of virtue, day in and day out, without the support of consolation.

| *For Reflection* | Where in my life do I struggle the most in doing God's will without the support of consolation? |

The Transition from Discursive Meditation to Contemplation

⌘

In John's day, the type of prayer common to beginners, through which God imparts consolation, was called discursive meditation. It is a systematic type of prayer that begins with the reading of a passage from the Gospels. Next, the imagination re-creates the Gospel scene in the mind. How detailed this pictorial representation will be is determined by the imaginative powers of the individual. For some souls it will be very clear and detailed, and for others it will be vague.

Next, the person reflects upon the image in his or her mind. This reflection produces spiritual thoughts. They, in turn, evoke feelings of affection. Finally, these sentiments of love find expression in words directed toward God. Discursive meditation is mental work. St. Teresa compared it to the labor of drawing water from a well (L.11.7).

John says that the first indication that a shift is taking place in a person's prayer life from discursive meditation to the initial stage of contemplative prayer (which we will define as a simple gazing upon God) is that the soul is unable to meditate discursively. "The first [sign] is the realization that one cannot make discursive meditation or receive satisfaction from it as before" (A.2.13.2).

But this sign is not a sufficient indication that God is at work, because the soul's inability to meditate may be due to other causes. For example, it may be the result of "dissipation or a lack of diligence" (A.2.13.6). In short, a person may not be able to meditate because he or she is beginning to lead a dissipated life. Because of laxity, the ability to do the work that discursive meditation demands has been lost.

In addition, there may be physical or emotional reasons for this inability to meditate; it could "be the product of some indisposition or melancholic humor" (N.1.9.2). We all know by experience how difficult it is to focus our minds when we are either physically sick or emotionally distraught; we can become so absorbed by pain or worry that the mental concentration that discursive meditation requires becomes almost impossible. But if the reason a soul cannot meditate is solely due to some physical or emotional indisposition, then, when the indisposition has passed, the ability to meditate will be restored. Since this indicates that the soul's inability to meditate may not be due to God's action, a second sign is needed.

The second sign is the soul's "disinclination" to meditate (A.2.13.3). Thus, not only does the soul have an inability to meditate (the first sign), but also it has no desire to do so. In fact, the soul finds the effort to meditate burdensome. "Dryness is now the outcome of fixing (*fijar*) the senses [the imagination] on subjects that formerly provided satisfaction" (A.2.13.2). *Fijar* means to fix as to fasten, to focus, to stare at, or to concentrate the mind upon. There is now an aversion to concentrate the mind on a specific object. "This effort of theirs [to meditate] is accompanied by an interior reluctance and repugnance" (N.1.10.1). Trying to meditate feels like a machine running without lubrication; it grinds on and on and on. The soul is weary of cranking out meditations. All it wants to do is to rest in a general awareness of God's presence, which is the third sign that indicates that God is drawing a soul out of discursive meditation into contemplative prayer. "The third and surest sign is that a person likes to remain alone in loving awareness of God, without particular considerations, in interior peace and quiet and repose, and without the acts and the exercises (at least discursive, those in which one progresses from point to point) of the intellect, memory and will. Such a one prefers to remain only in a general loving awareness and knowledge of God . . . without any particular knowledge or understanding" (A.2.13.4).

The person experiences the three signs as a threefold shift in prayer: I can't meditate. I don't want to meditate. All I want to do is to sit quietly in God's presence. John says that if all three signs are present together, then it is safe to discontinue discursive meditation.

I emphasize the word *discursive* because it is important to be clear that John is talking about a specific type of prayer that should be discontinued—prayer that "progresses from point to point" (A.2.13.4), an overly cognitive exercise that employs "discursive analysis and synthesis of ideas" (N.1.9.8).

So how should a soul pray that has discerned these three signs within itself?

John does not give a detailed answer to this question. Rather, he presents us with an overall attitude that we should adopt in prayer. "When spiritual persons cannot meditate, they should learn to remain in God's presence with a loving attention and a tranquil intellect" (A.2.15.5). In *The Dark Night*, John expands upon this advice: "The attitude necessary in this night of sense is to pay no attention to discursive meditation since this is not the time for it. . . . All that is required . . . is freedom of soul. . . . They must be content simply with a loving and peaceful attentiveness to God, and live without the concern, without the effort, and without the desire to taste or feel Him. All these desires disquiet the soul and distract it from the peaceful quiet, and sweet idleness of the contemplation that is being communicated to it" (N.1.10.4).

It is important to note that even though John tells us we should not force ourselves to meditate, he does not advocate that we should do nothing. We should be gently attentive to the presence of God, focusing the mind, without strain or undue exertion. Sometimes this loving and peaceful attentiveness is the result of God holding our attention. This is when prayer tends to be more passive (receptive) than active. "They will often find themselves in this loving or peaceful awareness without having first engaged in any active work . . . with their faculties; they will not be working actively but only receiving" (A.2.15.2). At other times, this attentiveness requires some effort on our part. "But on the other hand they will frequently find it necessary to aid themselves gently and moderately with meditations in order to enter this state" (A.2.15.2). Think of a bird hovering in flight. At times, all it needs to do is to spread its wings to catch the wind. But when the wind subsides, the bird will have to gently flap its wings to stay aloft. We are not in control of God any more than the bird controls the wind. We have to humbly submit and adjust our prayer to how God is present to us. But no matter how "active" our prayer, we are to meditate "gently and moderately."

John does not give a list of "aids" for meditation. This is where we have to fill in the blanks. The best advice I can give is to use what you find to be helpful to sustain your awareness of God during prayer. No two people pray alike. Some people will find it helpful to simply repeat a single word, such as Jesus, God, or Love. Others are more inclined to some form of *lectio divina.* Still others are helped by forming an image in their minds. (Using a mental image as an aid to focus the mind is not discursive meditation.) And some people find visual aids, such as icons or some sacred image or sitting before the Blessed Sacrament to be the most beneficial.

Regardless of the means, the goal should be the same. We "should learn to remain in God's presence with a loving attention and a tranquil intellect" (A.2.15.5). The soul's attitude that should be adopted in contemplative prayer may best be illustrated by the following story. St. John Vianney once asked an old peasant, who frequently sat quietly before the Blessed Sacrament, "What do you do when you sit there?" The peasant responded, "I look at Him, and He looks at me, and we are happy." This is an example of "a loving and peaceful attentiveness to God" (N.1.10.4).

For *Reflection*	Do I appreciate that simply being aware of God's presence is prayer? What do I find most helpful in sustaining my awareness of God's presence during prayer?

By Their Fruits
You Will Know Them

J ohn assures his readers that if they experience these three
signs simultaneously, it is safe to discontinue discursive
meditation. Nevertheless, he anticipates the following objec-
tion: are we not "wasting time and straying from the right
road" (A.2.14.4) since we are deprived of the nourishment
that we once derived from meditation? John would answer in
the negative. He would contend that contemplation nourishes
our souls, but the nourishment is of a more refined nature.

In one sense, the simple knowledge derived from contemplation is the distillation of meditation. "What the soul
gradually acquired through the labor of meditation . . . has
been converted into habitual and substantial, general loving
knowledge" (A.2.14.2). In short, by contemplation, souls
are nourished by the fruits of their labors. "The difference
[between meditation and contemplation] . . . is between
toil and the enjoyment of the fruits of this toil" (A.2.14.7).

In theory, this explanation should put to rest the above
misgiving. However, in practice, it often does not. This is
because the nature of the knowledge that contemplation
imparts is "so recondite and delicate" (A.2.14.8) that it is nearly
"imperceptible to the soul" (A.2.14.10). In consequence,

people who are gifted with contemplative prayer sometimes question whether they are praying at all, since they feel they are doing nothing. To quell this fear, John tells his readers that the soul occupied in contemplation *is* doing something; it is being receptive. God nourishes souls that both meditate discursively and contemplate; the former "conceives" knowledge, and the latter "receives" knowledge (A.2.14.6). But even with this explanation, doubts may persist.

So, John tells us that in the final analysis, the only way we can have certitude that we are not being idle during prayer, when we are not meditating discursively but only resting in a loving awareness of God's presence, is to examine our life outside of prayer. Look at "the effects it produces in the soul" (A.2.14.14). If we are growing in self-knowledge, virtue, and an awareness of God's presence in our daily life, then we can rest assured that all is well (see N 1.12–13 for the effects of contemplation on the soul).

> *For Reflection* John tells us that one of the principal fruits of contemplation is "a habitual remembrance of God" (N.1.13.4). What means have I found to be helpful in fostering this habitual remembrance of God?

The Obscure Certainty of Faith

T he subject matter of the second book of *The Ascent* is
faith. However, John is not concerned with the content or
articles of faith. Rather, his focus is on faith as contemplation:
the quiet, gentle presence of God that "instructs [the soul] in
the perfection of love without its doing anything or understanding how it happens" (N.2.5.1). Faith as contemplation
does not communicate facts about God but is an experience of
God's self-communication. "Faith . . . communicates God
Himself to us" (C.12.4).

Therefore, to grow in faith is to deepen our awareness of
and attentiveness to God's indwelling presence. It is a "habit of
soul" or a habitual state of consciousness (A.2.3.1). The knowledge that faith provides is intuitive. It is like peripheral vision;
we do not clearly see the object that is in the corner of our eye
but are certain that it is there. This is why John says that faith
"brings *certitude* to the intellect [but] does *not produce clarity*"
(A.2.6.2; italics added).

Allowing oneself to be led is the central act of faith for
John. The journey of faith is following that intuitive sense of
what God wants us to do; it is heeding the heart's still, quiet
voice; it's the willingness to relinquish control. "As regards this
road to union, entering on the road means leaving one's own
road" (A.2.4.5). This is what John means when he says that

faith is like a guide to a blind person. To live by faith is to be willing to be led and instructed by Another (A.2.4.2). What God instructs us in is "the perfection of love" (N.2.5.1).

For	In daily life, how do I experience God
Reflection	instructing me in the perfection of love?

The Voice of Faith
and the Voice of Reason

Besides following the voice of faith as contemplation, John tells us that we must also heed the voice of reason. "Be attentive to your reason in order to do what it tells you concerning the way to God" (SLL.44). John compares the relationship between faith and reason to the light of the sun (faith) that eclipses the light of the stars (reason). "The sun so obscures all other lights that they do not seem to be lights at all when it is shining" (A.2.3.1).

The light of faith eclipses the light of reason; it does not eradicate it. We need to attend to the voice of reason, but reason needs to be docile to the voice of faith. In short, even though we should listen to reason in discerning the will of God, it should not have the last word. For "reason [must be] ordered to God." (A.3.29.4). Reason that is not ordered to God is disordered. It is like a disciple who will not listen to the voice of his or her master.

When we do not want to listen to God, we defend ourselves with every pretext, every excuse, and every rationalization that we can muster. In such a situation, God does not leave us to our own devices. Think of a time when you instinctively knew that God was asking you to do something you did not want to do. Did you not try to avoid doing God's will by countering it with reasonable arguments? But no matter how reasonable your arguments, did not a voice deep within you oppose your reasoning? This is an experience of what John means when he writes that "faith nullifies (*negándola*) the light of the intellect" (A.2.3.4). The Spanish word *negar*, from which *negándola* is derived, means to prohibit, to oppose, or to veto. Thus, one of the ways that we experience God's presence is as a divine veto that nullifies our rationalizations so we may be instructed in the perfection of love.

For Reflection   Can I recall times when listening to God's vetoing voice has protected me from my own destructive rationalizations? Is there a behavior or relationship in my life that I am not at peace with because I am ignoring God's voice?

Like Trying to Explain Color
to a Blind Person

If those born blind were told about the nature of the colors white or yellow, they would understand absolutely nothing, no matter how much instruction they received. Since they never saw these colors nor others like them, they would not have the means to form a judgment about them. Only the names of these colors would be grasped since the names are perceptible through hearing; but never their form or image, because these colors were never seen by those born blind. Such is faith to the soul; it informs us of matters we have never seen or known. (A.2.3.2–3)

The above passage expresses two truths. First, the light of God's grace enables us to see a dimension of reality to which we were previously blind; we perceive life around us and within us from a divine perspective.

Second, grace not only transforms our vision of life but also radically alters what we value. In turn, our relationships with others are changed. Have you ever experienced the frustration of trying to share with someone a reality in your life that they do not value? Isn't it like trying to explain color to a blind person, as the old saying has it? Yes, the person you are talking to may understand what you're saying intellectually, but you instinctively know that they don't *really* understand.

This is because real communication is on the level of experience and shared values.

A few years after I entered the Carmelites, I went home on vacation. One night, while spending an evening with several of my high school classmates, one of them asked me, "So Marc, what do you do in that monastery?" After enumerating my various household tasks, I said, "But for the most part, we pray." My classmate courteously nodded his head but after an awkward pause said, "That's great, but what do you *do*?" The more I tried to explain the centrality of prayer in my Carmelite vocation, the more frustrated I became.

In the monastery, my classmate's question would never arise, for prayer was a corporate value of the group. Its importance was a given. When a value is shared between two people, no explanation is necessary; when it is absent, no explanation is possible.

When people don't share the same values, real communication breaks down. Thomas Green writes, "We will find it difficult to establish a common ground with people who view life purely naturalistically. Once the Lord has become very real and important to us, it will be difficult, if not impossible, to communicate with people to whom he means little or nothing. This is painful, since these people may be humanly close to us—family or longtime friends."[2]

There is a certain innate loneliness on the spiritual path. At times, we can feel that we are living with a secret we cannot share, even with those with whom we are most intimate. We feel like an outsider within a group of colleagues and feel that we have to leave a part of ourselves outside the room. It is an ache that never seems to go away, a loneliness that is hard to put into words. It is not a problem to be solved but part of the cross to be borne.

For Reflection

As grace transforms my vision of life and alters my values, have I experienced changes in my personal relationships? Have I ever considered that as painful as these changes may be, they are part of the cross that I am asked to bear?

Love Is Not Blind; It Gives Sight

⨳

In chapter 5 of book two of *The Ascent*, John discusses the nature of union with God. In doing so, he differentiates two types of union: substantial union and union of likeness. The first type of union refers to God's sustaining presence in our lives. "To understand the nature of this union, one should first know that God sustains every soul and dwells in it substantially, even though it may be that of the greatest sinner in the world. This union between God and creatures always exists. By it He conserves their being so that if the union should end they would immediately be annihilated and cease to exist. . . . God is ever present in the soul . . . and thereby bestows and preserves its natural being by His sustaining presence" (A 2.5.3–4).

The mystery that these words conceal is nothing less than awesome. They tell us that while God and creation are distinct from one another, creation is completely permeated and utterly saturated by God. Think of creation as a piece of iron that has been placed into fire (God) and left there until the iron glows. Or think of a ray of light (God) shining through water (creation). Just as the fire and the light interpenetrate every molecule of the iron and water respectively, so too, does God's sustaining presence interfuse with our being. Our very existence is so pervaded by God's presence that it is more

115

correct to assert that we *are* a relationship with God than to say we *have* a relationship with God.

Yet, as overwhelming as substantial union is, John's focus is on the union of likeness. This type of union occurs "when God's will and the soul's are in conformity . . . transformed in God through love . . . and to the soul that is more advanced in love, more conformed to the divine will, God communicates Himself more" (A.2.5.3–4). To illustrate the interrelationship between the soul's growth in love and its corresponding capacity to receive God's communications, John uses the image of different people viewing the same masterpiece of art.

> Let us imagine a perfect painting with many finely wrought details and delicate, subtle adornments, including some so delicate and subtle that they are not wholly discernible. Now one whose sense of sight is not too clear and refined will discover less detail and delicacy in the painting; one whose vision is somewhat purer will discover more details and perfections; and another with yet clearer vision will find still more perfection; finally, the one who possesses the clearest faculty will discern the greatest number of excellent qualities and perfections. There is so much to behold in the painting that no matter how much one sees in it, still more remains unseen. (A.2.5.9)

John's image of various people perceiving different depths of beauty as they gaze at the same painting is analogous to Harry and Clara who one night attended a performance of Schubert's Trout Quintet. Both thoroughly enjoyed the music, but what Clara heard was vastly different from what Harry heard. But how is this possible? They sat side by side, and both Clara and Harry had received glowing reports from their audiologist the previous week. But hearing is not merely a function of our ears. Our ears perceive vibrations, but hearing is a function of the whole person. Clara was able to hear nuances of the music to which Harry was deaf because Clara was a professional musician, whereas Harry was a computer programmer. Clara's musical training required her to listen attentively to music for hours on end. In consequence, Clara had the ability to hear sounds and nuances of sound inaccessible to the untrained ear.

In his image of the painting, John employs a similar metaphor in attempting to describe various degrees of union. Two people can look at the same painting but see different realities. One person will be able to see a depth of details and differentiate shades of color that another person cannot. What enables one person to see more in a painting than another person is similar to what makes it possible for Clara to hear nuances of sounds that Harry could not—a depth of perception. The question now arises, "What deepens our perception of God?" In one word, love. As St. Thomas teaches, "Where there is love there is vision."[3]

For Reflection

As I've grown in my capacity to love, how has my vision of life deepened? In what ways do the eyes of my soul view things differently than they have in the past?

Visions and Revelations

Up to this point in *The Ascent*, John's focus has been on one way that God communicates to us, namely, faith, through the "dark and general knowledge" called contemplation, which both enlightens our inner darkness and instructs us in the perfection of love. However, God can communicate to us by other means, such as visions, revelations, locutions, and other types of religious experience.

In John's writings, visions, and so forth, are classified according to the means through which they are communicated. For example, visions that come to us through the external senses are called corporeal. They are seen, heard, tasted, smelled, or felt by our bodily senses. Imaginative visions are fashioned from images recorded in our memory. Intellectual visions are communicated directly by God, bypassing both the external and internal (imagination) senses. Before we deal with John's teaching on these different types of communications, let us first describe them. For the sake of clarity, we will give examples of only the major categories of these communications without considering the various subdivisions.

CORPOREAL VISIONS

Regarding corporeal visions, John writes, "The supernatural knowledge that reaches the intellect by way of the exterior bodily senses . . . [can come through] visions of images and persons from the other life: saints, of the good and bad angels, and of unusual lights and splendors . . . [or] by hearing . . . extraordinary words . . . [or smelling] the sweetest fragrances, [or] by tasting very exquisite savors" (A.2.11.1).

The following is an example of these types of visions. Once, while praying that a friend would not offend God, St. Teresa said that she "heard a very gentle voice . . . with my *bodily ears* and . . . in this experience realized that what I had asked for would be accomplished. As a result it happened that my affliction left me completely" (L.39.3; italics added).

IMAGINARY VISIONS

Imaginary visions take place within the confines of the imagination, where God constructs visual representations from images and intelligible forms that dwell in the memory. They can impart wisdom or warn the recipient of spiritual danger (A.2.16.3). An example of the latter is the time that Christ appeared to St. Teresa, admonishing her to sever an unhealthy friendship. "With great severity, Christ appeared before me, making me understand what He regretted about the friendship. I saw Him with the eyes of my soul [imagination] more clearly than I could have with the eyes of my body. . . . I was left very frightened and disturbed, and didn't want to see that person any more" (L.7.6).

Corporeal and imaginative visions are similar in nature. The former come to us by means of the external senses; the latter by means of the internal senses (imagination). However, since imaginative visions are more interior, they are more spiritual. In consequence, "the effect produced [is] more subtle and effective in the soul" (A.2.16.3).

INTELLECTUAL VISIONS

There are two problems with the term "intellectual vision." The first is the word *intellectual*, and the second is the word *vision*. To describe these most interior and spiritual of all graces as "intellectual" is misleading, for the word carries with it connotations of study, reflection, and speculation. However, *intellectual*, as the word is used here, refers to knowledge that is communicated directly to the soul, without the instrumentality of either the external or the internal senses.

The word *vision* is problematic because John uses it metaphorically. It does not refer to a visual representation (even though a visual representation may be a part of an intellectual vision), but rather to the soul's intuitive grasp or apprehension of spiritual reality. "Let it be known that in a *broad sense* these . . . apprehensions can be titled visions of the soul because we also call the understanding of soul its vision" (A.2.23.2; italics added). John prefers the word *apprehensions* (*aprehensiones*) to *visions* because it more accurately expresses the essence of these types of divine communications, namely, that the soul both apprehends and is apprehended; it grasps and is grasped; and it seizes and is seized by God.

Intellectual apprehensions are the most interior types of visions. They carry with them a certitude that they are from God and are not a product of either the devil or our psyche. When St. Teresa was beginning to receive visions, she believed they were from God but was afraid they might be from the devil (a fear that was reinforced by her confessors). It was during this time of confusion and anguish that Teresa received her first intellectual vision that gave her the assurance that her visions were from God. "I felt Christ beside me; I saw nothing with my bodily eyes or with my soul [imagination], but it seemed to me that Christ was at my side—I saw that it was He. . . . It seemed to me that Jesus Christ was always present at my side; but since this wasn't an imaginative vision, I didn't see any form. Yet I felt very clearly that He was always present at my side and that He was the witness of everything I did. . . . At no time . . . was I able to ignore that He was present at my side" (L.27.2).

Teresa did not "see" Jesus but apprehended his presence. When Teresa's confessor asked her how she knew it was Jesus beside her, she responded, "I answered that I didn't know how, but that I couldn't help knowing that He was beside me, that I saw and felt Him clearly, that my recollection of soul was greater, and that I was very continuously in the prayer of quiet, that the effects were much different from those I usually experienced, and that it was very clear" (L.27.3).

Both the clarity and the depth of the spiritual effects of the vision gave Teresa the assurance that she needed. "It is impressed with such clear knowledge that I don't think it can be doubted. The Lord desires to be so engraved upon the intellect that this vision can no more be doubted than can what is seen. . . . Even though a suspicion may at first arise, there remains on the other hand such great certitude that the doubt has no force" (L.27.5).

LOCUTIONS

A locution (the Latin *locution*, derived from *loqui* meaning "to speak") is a type of intellectual apprehension, whereby the soul hears a word or words. There are different types of locutions, the most interior being "substantial locutions," which are words that are heard within the depths of the soul. They are efficacious words that produce what they signify. For example, if God says to the soul "Have no fear," great fortitude and tranquility are instantly given. Or if God says, "Be good," the soul "would immediately be substantially good" (A.2.31.1). Substantial locutions carry with them an assurance of authenticity. They are unmistakably from God; they cannot be either produced by our imagination or counterfeited by the devil. They have the quality of words that are heard and not composed, to use St. Teresa's comparison (IC.6.3.14).

JOHN'S TEACHING

It is a common misconception that John's stance on visions is purely negative. This is not true, for he recognizes them (especially the more interior ones) as great blessings, bestowed by God, that produce in the soul "quietude, illumination, happiness, resembling that of glory, delight, purity, love, humility and an elevation and inclination toward God" (A.2.24.6).

John's teaching on visions may best be described as cautionary. As an experienced spiritual director, he knew firsthand the spiritual damage that results when a person either misinterprets or becomes attached to an extraordinary spiritual experience. For John, the greatest potential danger of visions is a diminishment of faith, for the more a soul becomes preoccupied and enmeshed in visions, the less it attends to that "dark loving knowledge, which is faith that serves as a means of divine union" (A.2.24.4). Or to express this same truth another way, "If the soul desires to feed upon them [visions, etc.], the spirit and senses will be so occupied that a free and simple communication of spirituality will be impossible" (A.2.16.11).

In addition, esteeming visions can make a person prone to pride or vulnerable to the deceptions of the devil. It is in the light of all these dangers that John says we "must never rely on them or accept them . . . [but] rather flee from them completely and have no desire to examine whether they be good or bad" (A.2.11.2).

What? Should we flee from these spiritual communications without even attempting to discern their origin? Can John be serious? What if their origin is divine? Would we not be disrespectful to God by rejecting his gifts? Besides, would we not be depriving ourselves of many blessings? To all of these objections, John's answer is a resounding "No."

The reason we should not pay any attention to visions is that it is unnecessary to do so. This is because the grace of the vision is imparted immediately and automatically. John's insistence on this point is indicated by his repetition of this teaching: "It produces its effect in the spirit at the very moment of its perception, without any deliberation about wanting or not wanting it. . . . God produces its effects passively in the spirit" (A.2.11.6). "It is not necessary for a person to have the desire to accept them [for] at the very moment they are present in the imagination they also produce and infuse knowledge and love, or whatever God wants them to cause" (A.2.16.10). "[The effect] is communicated passively, exclusive of any effort of the soul to understand" (A.2.16.11).

John compares the grace of these divine communications to a red-hot poker, which leaves its mark on a person's skin, even if he or she is sleeping. In consequence, John teaches that it is unnecessary and potentially dangerous even to try to discern the origin of visions (God, the devil, or the psyche). "Individuals [should] free themselves from the task and danger of discerning the true visions from the false ones. . . . Such an effort is profitless, a waste of time, a hindrance to the soul, an occasion of many imperfections as well as of spiritual stagnancy" (A.2.17.7).

To sum up John's teaching, if you are a recipient of a vision, thank God for the gift that you have received. However, you should not become entangled in it, by either thinking about it or trying to discern its origin. To do so is both unnecessary and potentially dangerous.

SEEING WITHIN CONTEXT

The first thing we should realize about extraordinary graces is that they are not arbitrary graces. They fulfill specific needs that exist at the time they are given. We have seen three examples of this truth in the visions of St. Teresa that we have already examined. For example, St. Teresa's corporeal vision gave her the assurance that her friend would not offend God. Similarly, her imaginary vision of Christ, who appeared to her "with great severity," struck such fear in Teresa's heart that it gave her the strength and determination to sever her unhealthy friendship. Finally, when Teresa was filled with anguish, not knowing whether her visions were from God or the devil, God granted her an intellectual vision that imparted certitude that her visions were of divine origin. In these examples, we see how God deals with all of us. God gives us what we need for our spiritual growth.

For Reflection Have I ever received a grace from God that was of such intensity that it could be called a vision? Considering that visions are not arbitrary graces but are given for a specific purpose, can I recall the specific need that I had at the time I received it?

Just Talking

⁂

Even if the visions are from God, spiritual persons and their masters can suffer harm if they are very credulous about them. . . . The reason motivating me to enlarge on this subject is the want of discretion that I have noticed in some spiritual masters. . . . The method of some directors is sufficient to encumber souls receiving visions, or even lead them astray. They do not guide them along the path of humility. . . . Neither do these directors ground their disciples in faith, for they frequently make these visions a topic of conversation. Consequently, the individuals get the idea that their directors are setting store by their visions, and as a result they do the same and stay attached to them. . . . All this arises from the attitude and language the individuals observe in their directors in these matters. . . . The reason souls become so readily engrossed in visions must be the sensible aspect toward which humans have a natural bent. And since individuals are already attracted [to visions] it is enough to see in their director, or any other person, some esteem for these visions and they will acquire the same. . . . [In consequence] they think their visions are significant . . . and that God is giving them prominence. They go about feeling pleased and satisfied with themselves. . . . *The spirit of the disciple is secretly fashioned after that of the spiritual father. . . . If the spiritual father has such a bent toward revelations that they produce in his soul some effect or pleasure, he cannot avoid—even though unaware—affecting his disciples with this attitude and pleasure.* (A.2.18.1–6; italics added)

One of the criticisms leveled against Anton Chekhov's plays is that their settings are dull and commonplace. In response to this charge, Chekhov said, "Let things that happen onstage be just as complex and yet just as simple as they are in life. For instance, people are having a meal at a table, just having a meal, but at the same time their happiness is being created, or their lives are being destroyed."[4] Thus, the very criticism leveled against Chekhov manifests one of the sources of his genius—his ability to disclose the human drama that is being enacted within the context of daily life.

Now, read the quoted passage from *The Ascent* as if it were a scene taken from one of Chekhov's plays. Two people are talking to one another, just talking. A young woman is speaking to a priest about some visions that she has recently received. The priest encourages the woman to tell him about them. Picking up on the priest's eagerness, the young woman shares her experiences in detail. The more she shares, the more the priest smiles and nods his head in approval. She picks up on his approval by means of his nonverbal and verbal cues, that is, by his "attitude and language" (A.2.18.2).

We see two people talking, just talking, but the real drama that is taking place is invisible to the eye. Imperceptibly, a transformation is taking place within the young woman, for "the spirit of the disciple is *secretly* (*secretamente*) fashioned after that of the spiritual father" (A.2.18.5; italics added). The transformation takes place secretly because it is hidden to both the outside observer and the young woman herself. She is unaware of the changes that are being secretly fashioned within her soul. She is not conscious that her director's attitudes are becoming her own; she is beginning to interpret her own experiences through his eyes, and she is blind to the damage this is causing. She is becoming attached to her visions, and her humility is being eroded.

John's teaching on spiritual directors is a cautionary tale, for "many spiritual masters cause great harm to a number of souls" (F.3.31). His message is clear: Be careful to whom you bare your soul. "Take care into whose hands [you] entrust [yourself]" (F.3.30).

For
Reflection

How would I describe the effect that my spiritual director has had on me?

The Atmosphere We Create

I n our previous reflection, we dealt with the harm that can
be done if a director makes the visions of his or her directees the focus of their conversations. However, we should not
conclude that John is saying that a director should never allow
directees to talk about their visions or other spiritual graces
they have received. In fact, John teaches that harm can be
done if a director forbids directees to talks about them. Here,
John is referring to directors who are "frightened (*espantarse*)
or scandalized (*escandalizarse*)" by visions (A.2.22.19).

Espantarse, derived from *espantar*, can mean to become
frightened. *Escandalizarse*, derived from *escandalizar*, can
mean to be scandalized or irritated by. In short, John is saying
that the director's negative reactions of fear, irritation, or anger
can make it impossible for a directee to speak about his or her
spiritual experiences.

This can be detrimental for two reasons. First, if a person
doesn't have the freedom to speak about a grace she or he has
received, the effect of the grace may be hindered. "The effect,
light, strength, and security of many divine communications
are not completely confirmed in a soul . . . until it discusses them with one whom God has destined to be spiritual
judge over it. . . . We witness [that] humble recipients of
these experiences obtain new satisfaction, strength, light, and

security after consulting about them with the proper person. This is so true that to some it seems that these communications neither take root nor belong to them until they confer about them and that the communications are then seemingly imparted anew" (A.2.22.16).

The importance of this statement goes far beyond visions and supernatural graces. How often do we need to go to another person and "check out" our experiences? And until we do, we can be plagued with doubts. Have we interpreted our experience correctly? Is our thinking distorted? Are we missing something? And it's not until a trusted person has confirmed the validity of the grace we have received that we can be at peace. And the peace allows us to fully experience the grace.

The second reason it may be detrimental to a soul not to be able to speak about a grace it has received is that it may be deprived of needed instruction. "A soul ordinarily needs instruction pertinent to its experience in order to be guided through the dark night" (A.2.22.17). John anticipates that this statement may cause his readers confusion since in a previous chapter he put great stress on rejecting visions. Therefore, he makes the following distinction. John says that giving needed instruction on visions is completely different from "making them a topic of conversation" (A.2.22.19). The former is for the sake of guidance; the latter is for the sake of satisfying curiosity.

In our previous reflection, we considered spiritual directors who are overeager to listen to their directees' accounts of their visions. Here, we are considering the opposite problem, namely, directors who are so opposed to talking about visions that they "forbid souls from making them a topic of conversation" (A.2.22.19). Such directors are so adamant in this regard that if one of their directees begins to broach the subject of visions, this person is treated with "severity, displeasure, or scorn" (A.2.22.19). John says that this attitude will "close the door to these souls, and cause them many difficulties (*inconvenientes*)" (A.2.22.19). *Inconvenientes* refer to difficulties as obstacles, obstructions, or impediments, a "closed door," as John suggests.

The major obstacle, as we mentioned above, is that the soul is unable to benefit from the grace received. However, there may be other difficulties that John had in mind. As the starting point of our exploration of these difficulties, let us recall John's assertion that "the spirit of the disciple is secretly fashioned after that of the spiritual father" (A.2.18.5). If directees "go about feeling pleased and satisfied with themselves" as a result of their director "setting store by their visions" (A.2.18.2), how might a directee feel whose director is frightened by visions and, whenever the subject is mentioned, treats the person with "severity, displeasure, or scorn" (A.2.22.19)? Wouldn't the directee begin to feel afraid and paint fearful scenarios in his or her imagination? "Are my visions hallucinations? Are they caused by the devil?"

So what is John's advice to spiritual directors? How can a director allow directees to speak freely about their visions without giving the impression that he or she is setting store by them? John answers this question as follows:

> Since God is leading them by this means [visions], there is no reason to oppose it or become frightened or scandalized over it. The spiritual father should instead proceed with much kindness and calm. He should give these souls encouragement and the opportunity to speak about their experiences. . . . [Then] spiritual directors should guide them in the way of faith by giving them good instructions

on how to turn their eyes from all these things and on their obligation to denude their appetite and spirit of these communications in order to advance. They should explain how one act done in charity is more precious in God's sight than all the visions and communications possible—since these imply neither merit nor demerit—and how it is that many individuals who have not received these experiences are incomparably more advanced than others who have received many. (A.2.22.19)

The first thing that John says a director should do is to create a welcoming environment of kindness (*benignidad*) and calmness (*sosiego*; A.2.22.19). *Benignidad* includes the qualities of kindness, graciousness, and courtesy, whereas *sosiego* means to be calm, quiet, and composed. The atmosphere created by these qualities provides a nonthreatening environment that is in stark contrast to the one created by directors who treat their directees with "severity, displeasure, or scorn" (A.2.22.19). It allows directees to speak freely without fear of being ridiculed or rejected. After the directee has spoken of his or her visions, the director is now in a position to provide guidance.

Once the director has affirmed the directee's vision as a grace given by God, "since God is leading them by these means," then the director can help the directee see these graces within context (A.2.22.19). "[Directors] should explain how one act done in charity is more precious in God's sight than all the visions and communications possible—since these imply neither merit nor demerit—and how it is that many individuals *who have not received* these experiences are incomparably *more advanced* than others who have received many" (A.2.22.19; italics added). This explanation is both an antidote to pride and an exhortation to set one's heart on the greater gifts—"and the greatest of these is love" (1 Cor 13:13).

<table>
<tr><td>For Reflection</td><td>In my conversations with others, do I create a welcoming environment of kindness and calmness in which people feel they may speak freely, or do my feelings create a barrier to communication?</td></tr>
</table>

The Wisdom of the Community

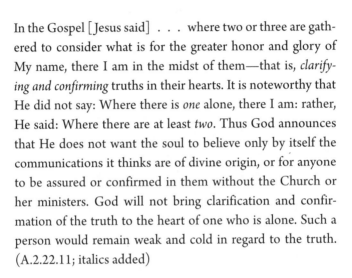

In the Gospel [Jesus said] . . . where two or three are gathered to consider what is for the greater honor and glory of My name, there I am in the midst of them—that is, *clarifying and confirming* truths in their hearts. It is noteworthy that He did not say: Where there is *one* alone, there I am: rather, He said: Where there are at least *two*. Thus God announces that He does not want the soul to believe only by itself the communications it thinks are of divine origin, or for anyone to be assured or confirmed in them without the Church or her ministers. God will not bring clarification and confirmation of the truth to the heart of one who is alone. Such a person would remain weak and cold in regard to the truth. (A.2.22.11; italics added)

This passage, even though it deals specifically with souls who have received visions and revelations, is pertinent to all of us, for it contains a basic truth, namely, that we are not always the best interpreters of our own experience. St. Teresa taught that it is one grace to receive a grace from God and another grace to correctly understand the grace that one has received (L.154). And the grace of understanding is often communicated to us through another person.

John does not say that we need someone to tell us the truth but that we need a trusted guide who is able to assist us in "clarifying (*aclarando*) and confirming (*confirmando*) truths

[that] are in [our] hearts." *Aclarando* is the process of clearing up obscurity or shedding light upon things that are unclear, whereas *confirmando* means to confirm and give support.

Good spiritual directors are hard to come by, you may say. This is true. However, the guidance of which John speaks can come to us through many sources. We can receive clarification and confirmation about the truths that are in our hearts from our spouse, a coworker, a support group, a friend, or even a book.

For Reflection	What are the channels through which I receive spiritual guidance? What or who is most helpful in clarifying or shedding light upon my experiences?

BOOK THREE

The Memory

John tells us that his exposition on the memory and hope "will be brief" because what he has to say has already been said in his consideration of the intellect and faith (A.3.1.1). Also, John's audience in his treatment of the purification of the intellect and memory is the same: those advancing in contemplation (A.3.2.1). In consequence, his advice regarding the person's relationship to the contents of both the intellect and the memory is the same: do not become entangled in them, so that the soul can attend to the presence of God. We must "learn to silence and quiet the faculties so that God may speak" (A.3.3.4).

After this introduction, John writes of what happens to the memory when a person experiences certain mystical graces, called "touches of union" (A.3.2.5). What John says regarding "touches of union" has frequently been misinterpreted because of the language he uses in describing them. John writes, "There is no way to union with God without *annihilating the memory* as to all forms" (A.3.2.4; italics added). Taken literally, these words sound as if John is saying that as a soul approaches divine union, everything recorded on the hard drive of our memory is erased, and the soul is left in a state of mental oblivion. Such an erroneous interpretation is strengthened by the following sentences: "Then owing to the union, the memory is emptied and purged of all knowledge, as I say, and remains in oblivion" (A.3.2.5). "Forms and knowledge are gradually being erased from the memory" (A.3.2.8).

John is describing a temporary condition of mental absorption. He is referring to a soul that is so inwardly absorbed and captivated by an overwhelming experience of God that it is oblivious to everything else. For the sake of understanding, let us make an analogy between the state that John is describing and the experience of grief.

Whenever we suffer a great loss, for example, the death of a loved one, we become mentally absorbed. At times, our preoccupation can be so intense that we are not fully present to the external world. In consequence, we often forget appointments and daily duties. Similarly, John says that when a soul has a deep experience of God's presence, it is "lost in great forgetfulness" because "it is absorbed in a supreme good [God]" (A.3.2.4). "This abstraction and oblivion is caused by the interior recollection in which this contemplation absorbs the soul" (N.2.8.2). Similarly, just as the memory of a person who has worked through his or her grief is restored, so too, when a soul has reached union with God, its lapses of memory cease. "Yet once the habit of union is attained one no longer experiences these lapses of memory" (A.3.2.8).

But for the soul that has reached union, its memory is not merely restored to its former state; it is transformed and has been divinized. This means that a soul in union remembers and forgets according to the mind of God. John provides the following examples:

> Here are some examples of these divine operations. A person will ask a soul in this state for prayers. The soul will not remember to carry this request through any form or idea

remaining in the memory. But if it is expedient to pray for this one, God will move the soul's will and impart a desire to do so; at times God will give it a desire to pray for others whom it has never known or heard of. The reason is that God alone moves these souls toward those works that are in harmony with His will and ordinance and they cannot be moved toward others. Thus the works and prayer of these souls always produce their effect. . . . Another example: At a particular time one will have to attend to a necessary business matter. There will be no remembrance through any form, but, without one's knowing how, the time and suitable way of attending to it will be impressed on the soul without fail. (A.3.2.10–11)

Why does a person who is united to God remember and forget according to the will of God? For the same reason that we tend to remember and forget things in daily life: we remember what is important to us and forget what is not. For example, if we are looking forward to having lunch with our best friend, the energy of desire makes it impossible for this appointment to slip from our minds. Conversely, we often forget what is unimportant to us because there is not enough psychic energy invested in it to keep it in our consciousness. In a similar way, if our will is united to God's, then what is important to God is important to us, and what is unimportant to God is unimportant to us. Thus, we remember and forget according to the will of God.

A transformed memory is purely the work of God. Nevertheless, we can dispose ourselves to God's transforming grace. Now, since what we remember and what we forget is influenced by our desire, we should ask the following question: what things does God want me to remember but I want to forget? For example, one of my community assignments is to clean the first-floor bathrooms in the monastery, which is not one of my favorite pastimes. In consequence, I frequently "forget" to do so.

Knowing that I want to forget, I have developed the practice of taping notes on the mirror above my sink: "Monday: do bathrooms." It is hard to forget something that stares me in the face. The note is a goodwill offering. It is a choice to try to remember what I want to forget.

For Reflection	What "goodwill" offerings could help me to remember what I want to forget?

Do Not Store Up
in the Memory

ince John is dealing with the active night of the memory in *The Ascent*, he tells us that he "will treat only of the manner in which, through the person's *own efforts*, the memory must be brought into this night and purgation" (A.3.2.14; italics added). In this regard, John offers a discipline pertaining to memory.

> We are imparting instructions here for advancing in contemplation to union with God. All these sensory means and exercises of the faculties [discursive meditation] must be left behind and in silence so that God Himself may effect divine union in the soul. As a result one has to follow this method of disencumbering, emptying, and depriving the faculties of their *natural authority* and operations to make room for the inflow and illumination of the supernatural. Those who do not turn their eyes from their natural capacity will not attain so lofty a communication; rather they will hinder it. (A.3.2.2; italics added)

A cursory reading of this passage has given rise to the belief that John is saying the memory has to be emptied, in the sense that its contents have to be erased. This is not what John is saying. The faculties of the intellect, memory, and will are not annihilated; rather, their use is restricted. Souls advancing in contemplation should "deprive the faculties of their natural authority (*jurisdicción*) and operations." Thus, John is saying that souls advancing in contemplation should restrict the jurisdiction on how and when they use the intellect, memory, and will.

John's counsel regarding restricting the authority of the memory is as follows: "The spiritual person should ordinarily take this precaution: Do not store up (*archivo*) objects of hearing, sight, smell, taste, or touch in the memory, but leave them immediately and forget them (A.3.2.14).

John sets before us a basic choice. What do we do when we experience something in our environment? Do we "store up (*archivo*) objects of hearing, sight, smell, taste, or touch in the memory," or do we "leave them immediately and forget them" (A.3.2.14)? That is, do we brood over what we see and hear as an old archivist (*archivo*) would mull over dusty tomes of ancient history, or do we choose not to dwell on our experiences? The following story illustrates this basic choice.

Once, two monks came to a river where a young woman, wary of crossing, was standing. The older monk offered his assistance and carried her across the river on his back. After he set her down on the other side, the two monks continued their journey in silence. The younger monk was very disturbed and preoccupied regarding what he had just witnessed. Many hours later he erupted with indignation: "How could you do such a thing! Our training tells us to avoid contact with women, but you picked her up and carried her." The old monk replied, "Yes, but I set her down at the river bank. Why are you still carrying her?"

The older monk practiced John's admonition to "leave immediately and forget," to "set down" so to speak, the objects of hearing, sight, smell, taste, or touch. The younger monk "stored up" what he had seen.

Lest we misinterpret John's admonition to "leave . . . immediately and forget" the contents of memory to mean that we should neither think about nor recall things to mind, we need to remember that John lived in a real world and knew the importance of the memory and the necessity of thinking (A.3.2.14). He writes, "People are not required to stop recalling and thinking about what they must do and know" (A.3.15.1). But what John does advocate is that we cease unnecessary thinking and that we do not willfully recall images and experiences to mind that distract us from God. "They should not think or look on these things [of the memory] *for longer than is sufficient* for the understanding and fulfillment of their obligations" (A.3.15.1; italics included).

For Reflection	In what way am I like the younger monk? What experiences in daily life do I tend to dwell on? How does such rumination affect me? Have I ever experienced the relief of being able to "set down" my preoccupations?

The Hair Trigger of Memory

W hy, we might ask, is it important not to dwell on the contents of the mind for longer than is sufficient? The obvious answer is to quiet the clamor of the mind, so we can hear the voice of God. However, there is another reason, based on the fact that what we see, hear, taste, smell, and feel is constantly setting in motion chains of mental associations. "Our nature is so unstable and fragile that, even when well disciplined, the memory will hardly fail to stumble (*tropezar*) on things that disturb the soul that was living in peace and tranquility through forgetfulness to all" (A.3.6.4). *Tropezar* can mean to stumble, to slip, to meet accidentally, or to bump into. In short, our memory has a hair trigger.

Picture yourself sitting at your desk paying your monthly bills. All of a sudden, you find yourself thinking of a person whom you used to date when you were in high school. The mental image of this person carries with it feelings of tenderness, sadness, affection, a sense of loss, sexual arousal, and so forth. These feelings interfuse with one another and create a bittersweet mood of nostalgia. This mood, in turn, triggers other memories. These memories alter your mood slightly and trigger additional memories. It is as if you are floating down a river in which the current steers you down various tributaries, one after another.

Our senses are constantly bumping into things that jar loose images from our memories. John tells us that this happens even to the well-disciplined soul that is at peace. Even in solitude we are not alone. We all have what John calls an "interior tongue" by which we carry on the conversations with ourselves (Pre.9). These conversations are triggered by images that arise from the memory. We find an example of this in the writings of the sixth-century monk St. John Climacus: "Once, while engaged on some task, I happened to be sitting outside a monastery and near the cells of those living in solitude. I could overhear them raging alone in their cells and in their bitter fury leaping about like caged partridges, leaping at the face of their offender as if he were actually there."[1]

When our interior tongue is unbridled, our passions, like a herd of wild horses, can run roughshod over our minds and rob us of our peace. It is impossible to preserve our peace and tranquility unless we attempt to discipline the memory. John writes,

> The soul is incapable of truly acquiring control of the passions and restriction of the inordinate appetites without forgetting and withdrawing from the sources of these emotions. Disturbances never arise in a soul unless through the apprehensions of the memory. When all things are forgotten, nothing disturbs the peace or stirs the appetites. As the saying goes: What the eye doesn't see, the heart doesn't want. We experience this all the time. We observe that as often as people begin to think about some matter, they are moved and aroused over it, little or much, according to the kind of apprehension. If the apprehension is bothersome and annoying, they feel sadness or hatred, and so on; if agreeable, they experience desire and joy, and so on. (A.3.5.1–2)

In this passage, John sets before us a basic truth. One of the greatest sources of stress in life is our inability to shut down the memory. How peaceful our lives would be if we had our memories and imaginations under control. So much of our trouble begins in the swirl of our thoughts. As Brother Lawrence of the Resurrection puts it, "Our thoughts spoil everything; that's how trouble starts."[2] Thus, John admonishes us not to "begin to *think*" about what the memory and imagination set before us. We cannot prevent memories and images from arising in our minds, but we need to do our best not to dwell on them. There is no other path to true peace.

For Reflection

There is a Chinese proverb that says we cannot stop the birds of worry and care from flying about our heads, but we can prevent them from building nests in our hair. Likewise, we cannot stop memories from arising in our mind, but we can choose not to dwell on them. What practices have I found helpful in preventing me from dwelling on memories that arise in my mind?

The Stomach of the Mind

The reason disturbances arise in a soul through the apprehensions of the memory is because what is recorded in memory is the whole event, what happened and how it felt. A memory is like a movie. What happened is comparable to the images that we see on the screen. How it felt is like the movie's emotionally laden soundtrack.

Whenever a memory arises in our mind, we also experience the emotion that clings to it. Also, every time we recall a memory and rehash it in our minds, the emotion that clings to it increases. "If they turn their memory to the objects of hearing, sight, touch, smell, and taste . . . some emotion will cling to them, whether it be sorrow, or fear, or hatred, vain hope, vain joy, or vainglory, and so on" (A.3.3.3).

John puts before us a vicious cycle. When our minds ruminate over an event, the images and emotions that thinking generates are stored in the memory. Because these memories are emotionally charged, they are easily triggered to the conscious mind. We are presented with a horrid example of this vicious cycle in Dante's *Inferno*. Count Ugolino and Archbishop Ruggieri are frozen together up to their necks in ice. Ugolino, who is situated behind Ruggieri, makes a gruesome meal of Ruggieri; he gnaws upon his head and neck. As Dante and Virgil come upon this horror, Ugolino raises his blood-stained mouth from his gory repast, wipes it upon his victim's hair, and recounts how Ruggieri had betrayed him. Ugolino tells the heartrending account of how Ruggieri had walled up him and his children in a tower and left them to starve to death. The retelling of his grief only increases Ugolino's rage. "His eyes narrowed to slits when he was done, and he seized the skull once again between his teeth grinding it as a mastiff grinds a bone."[3]

Ugolino's story elicits our pity, but his is an edited tale. Ugolino fails to mention the part he played in his tragic end: how he had been a coconspirator with Ruggieri in betraying his own family for the sake of political advancement. Ruggieri's treachery was but the final tragic twist in Ugolino's own life of treachery and deceit.

Our memory is like Ugolino's tale. It is self-serving. It edits the events of our past according to our needs. This is because the memory does not operate independent of the will, which edits out facts that we want to forget and embellishes those we want to remember. Just as the history of a people is not a record of events but an interpretation of events, so too is memory to the individual. What is recorded in memory is not what happened but what we believe happened. Every time we recount the past, we revise it in some way. The ink that rewrites our tales is the emotions that we experience in the process of recalling the past.

The grief Ugolino experiences as he recounts his final days transforms him into an innocent victim full of exonerating self-pity and justifiable rage. The same is true for us. When the memory, what St. Augustine calls "the stomach of the mind,"[4] regurgitates the past, "some emotion will cling [to us], whether it be sorrow, or fear, or hatred, vain hope, vain joy, or vainglory, and so on," that "contaminates the soul" (A.3.3.3). The emotional atmosphere of the soul becomes polluted. Thinking and feeling mutually reinforce and feed off one another in a vicious cycle. To use John's language, when "the memory focuses on (*revuelve*)" what the will desires, we keep the past alive. *Revuelve*, derived from *revolver*, means to turn over in one's mind or to retrace (A.1.9.6). Like Count Ugolino, the more we chew upon the past, the greater the intensity of emotion that clings to and contaminates our soul.

John warns us that this process happens "subtly" (*sutilísimamente*), that is, gradually and with great cunning (A.3.3.3). In this regard, we need to pay careful attention to dwelling on past injuries, especially when we feel that our anger is justified. We have an example of this in the life of St. Augustine. A scandal arose when Augustine was nominated to be a bishop. Bishop Megalius, the senior bishop of Numidia, publicly accused Augustine of seducing a married woman with a love potion. The story was pure slander, and the recklessness of Megalius's accusation infuriated Augustine. On the occasion of Megalius's death, Augustine wrote to Profuturus, a fellow bishop, and took the opportunity to reflect upon the danger of nursing justifiable anger.

> We must be on guard lest hatred for anyone should seize our innermost heart and prevent us from "praying to God in our chamber, having shut the door," for you know quite well that hatred would close the door against God Himself. Anger creeps in so subtly that everyone thinks that his own anger is just, and habitual anger becomes hatred. And the mingled sweetness of a just resentment is like a trace of perfume in a vial, remaining too long until the whole becomes sour and the vial unfit for use. Therefore, it is better not for us to harbor even a just anger against

anyone, because it is only too easy to fall unperceived from just anger into hatred.[5]

Resentment lingers in the soul because it sounds like the voice of reason and justice, sweet with the morose pleasure of self-pity. Over time, the emotion no longer clings to us; we cling to it.

For Reflection	In the stomach of my mind is there a memory over which I ruminate? What effect has this had on my spiritual development?

Tranquility of Soul

❧

The two main powers of memory are our capacities to remember and to forget. Both are necessary to function in this world. If we could not remember, we would not be able to recognize or identify any person or object, and words would be reduced to sounds devoid of meaning. Conversely, if we could not forget, that is, if everything recorded in our psyches were present to our conscious mind, we would be flooded and bombarded with thoughts, images, and sense impressions. Our nervous system would be so overstimulated by the overload of our minds that we would break down.

In chapter 6 of book three of *The Ascent*, John concludes his treatment of the natural knowledge recorded in memory by enumerating the benefits derived from mortifying the memory and the imagination, chief among them being tranquility of soul.

This tranquility of soul is the ability to forget, that is, to disengage one's mind and to mentally walk away from a situation. "People would never lose this tranquility if they were to forget ideas and lay aside (*dejase*) their thoughts" (A.3.6.4). *Dejase*, derived from *dejar*, can mean to lay aside, to leave behind, or to put down. But no matter how we translate *dejase*, the meaning contained in the image is the peace that comes from the ability to close the door of our minds to the outside world. This is the fruit of "disencumbering, emptying, and depriving the faculties of their natural authority (*jurisdicción*)" (A.3.2.2).

Tranquility of mind is the ability to establish mental borders, to set up jurisdictions. It is having a place for everything and having everything in its place. As St. Augustine puts it, "Peace is the order of tranquility . . . a pattern which assigns to each thing its *proper* position" (italics added).[6] There is a time to think and reflect, and there is a time to quiet one's mind. John underscores the great blessing of this peace by contrasting it with a mind that is afflicted with useless worry: "Even though no other benefit would come through this oblivion and void of the memory than freedom from afflictions and disturbances, it would be an immense advantage and blessing for a person. For the afflictions and disturbances engendered in a soul through adversities are no help in remedying these adversities; rather, distress and worry ordinarily make things worse and even do harm to the soul itself. Thus David proclaimed: 'Indeed every human being is disturbed in vain' [Ps. 39:6]" (A.3.6.3).

We all know the truth contained in this passage. Worry accomplishes nothing and actually makes things worse. It deprives us of thinking with a calm mind and robs us of the peace of God's presence. For an "unsettled soul" is the result of an "encumbered (*embarazada*) memory" (A.3.5.3). Within the context of this passage, *embarazada* may best be interpreted as entangled or cumbersome. It refers to a mind that is entangled in thought and weighed down with worry.

The opposite of this haggard state of consciousness is a soul that rests in "oblivion (*olvido*) and void (*vacio*) of the memory" (A.3.6.3). *Olvido* can be translated as "to forget," and *vacio* can mean unoccupied or disengaged. How do we disengage our minds from useless worry? John offers a helpful perspective: "Clearly, it is always vain to be disturbed, since being disturbed is never any help. Thus *if the whole world were to crumble and come to an end and all things were to go wrong*, it would be useless to get disturbed, for this would do more harm than good" (A.3.6.3; italics added). This perspective of being undisturbed as the whole world crumbles about oneself must have resonated deeply with John's soul, for he reflected upon it more than once in his writings: "And in order to preserve your tranquility of soul, *even if the whole world crumbles* you should not desire to advert to these things or interfere, remembering Lot's wife who was changed into hard stone because she turned her head to look at those who in the midst of much clamor and noise were perishing [Gn 19:26]" (Co.2; italics added). "[So that] the spirit be preserved . . . there is no better remedy than . . . through the inclination toward and practice of solitude and forgetfulness of all creatures and happenings, *even though the whole world crumbles*" (Lt.8; italics added).

John may have used the image of the world crumbling about him as a means of disengaging his memory from useless worry. This enabled him to dwell in the quiet spaciousness of holy solitude, where he could commune with God.

For Reflection	Like John, have I found an image or perspective that helps me to disengage my mind from useless worry and achieve tranquility of soul?

Supernatural Knowledge
in the Memory

I n book two of *The Ascent*, John dealt with how the soul
should relate to supernatural experiences (visions, locutions, etc.) that it is receiving. In book three, beginning with
chapter 7, John deals with how the individual should relate to
visions that have been received, that is, those that are recorded
in memory. Visions received in the past still exert an influence
upon us. "They usually leave an image, form, figure or idea
impressed either in the soul or in the memory" (A.3.7.1).

Because visions, whether they are present tense or past
tense, are fundamentally the same reality, John's advice to the
soul in relating to them is the same. Don't be attached to
them because they can do you harm. The reason a person
becomes attached to spiritual experiences recorded in the
memory is identical to why beginners become attached to
consolation: pleasure. "There are many who do not want to
go without the sweetness and delight of this knowledge in
the memory" (A.3.7.2).

What John says in chapters 7 through 12 of book three,
where he deals with supernatural knowledge recorded in the
memory, parallels what he said about visions in book two of
The Ascent. If the soul becomes attached to the knowledge of

spiritual experiences that are recorded in memory, its attention is diverted from the contemplation that God is communicating to it. In consequence, the soul's union with God is hindered (A.3.11). Also, the soul runs the risk of deception (A.3.8), presumption (A.3.9), and interference from the devil (A.3.10) and forms inadequate concepts about God (A.3.12). Let us explore this last harm, since we have dealt with the others in previous reflections.

All of our thoughts, concepts, and images about God are inadequate, whether they are derived from thinking, reading, or profound supernatural experiences. This is because God "is incomparable and incomprehensible" (A.3.12.1). This fact cannot be changed, for a finite mind can never understand an infinite God. However, John is concerned about what happens to the soul that has too high an estimation of its image of God.

In writing about supernatural apprehensions that are recorded in the memory, John says that "the *desire* of preserving" them shapes the soul's concept of God and that the soul is unaware that this is happening. "Though one may not form *an explicit* idea that God is similar to these apprehensions, nevertheless *the very esteem* for them . . . *produces* in the soul an *estimation* and *opinion* of God" (A.3.12.1; italics added).

This passage raises several questions. Why do I want to preserve my image of God? What need does it fulfill? For example, is my image of an all-merciful God in the service of maintaining a seriously sinful habit? I tell myself, "I have nothing to fear because no matter what I do, God will always forgive me." Conversely, do I find comfort in my image of a strict God of justice because it provides me with a false sense of security? Does it give me the certitude of knowing where I stand with God? Does it make the spiritual life black and white? "In order to avoid going to hell, all I need to do is to avoid committing mortal sins. And if I avoid certain behaviors, I'm safe." Also, such a concept of God risks reducing the spiritual life to keeping the commandments. This relieves a person from the obligation of responding to the promptings of the Spirit.

For Reflection What is my image of God? How does it function in my life? Does it help me to be open to the promptings of God's Spirit, or does it protect me from what God is asking me to do?

Remembrance of Things Past

Our previous reflection raises an important question. Is there a proper esteem that we can have for spiritual experiences recorded in the memory? Can it be beneficial for a person to call to mind a spiritual experience recorded in memory? John would say, "Yes." He writes,

> Only for the sake of moving the spirit to love should the soul at times recall the images and apprehensions that produced love. The effect produced by the remembrance of this communication is not as strong as the effect at the time the communication was received, yet when the communication is recalled there is a renewal of love and an elevation of the mind to God (A 3.13.6). . . . This knowledge may be remembered when it produces a good effect, *not in order to retain it but to awaken the knowledge and love of God*. But if the remembrance produces no good effect, the soul should never desire the memory of it. (A.3.14.2; italics added)

This passage focuses on the different motives that a soul can have for calling to mind past spiritual experiences. Is it for the sake of retaining the sweetness they produce or to strengthen the soul to do the will of God? Although, in this passage, John is referring to supernatural graces that are recorded in the memory, we can apply his teaching to anything that is recorded in memory. If calling to mind a past event helps to strengthen your resolve against temptation, soften your judgments against your neighbor, or inspire you to love, then by all means do so. John's criteria of what is permissible for us to call out of memory may be summed up by the Gospel criteria "You will know them by their fruits" (Mt 7:20). Or as John puts it, does "it produce a good effect" (A.3.14.2)?

John's teaching on our relationship to spiritual experiences recorded in the memory is a further exposition of his main teaching that we have seen throughout *The Ascent*. All things are good and are meant to be means to lead us to God but can become obstacles if we take up the wrong relationship to them. If we call to mind a spiritual experience for the sake of experiencing spiritual sweetness, it will become an obstacle to union with God because an attachment to spiritual sweetness will have been formed. However, calling to mind the same experience for the sake of growing in love of God and neighbor is not only permissible but also encouraged by John. "But for knowledge of the Creator, I declare that a person *should strive to remember* it as often as possible because it will produce in the soul a notable effect" (A.3.14.2; italics added).

For Reflection	John's teaching on why it is permissible to call to mind past spiritual experiences is applicable to anything recorded in memory. What past events, images, or ideas, when called to mind, awaken my love for God?

The Will

❧

T he final section of *The Ascent* deals with "the purification
of the will through charity" (A.3.16.1). John says that
the goal is nothing less than the fulfillment of the great com-
mandment to love God with our whole heart, soul, will, and
strength. As in the previous two sections, John will be dealing
with the active night, that is, the choices that are necessary to
"form and perfect the virtue of the charity of God" (A.3.16.1).
To achieve this goal, the will must "turn away from (*desvía*) all
that is not God" (A.3.16.2). *Desvía*, derived from *desviar*, can
mean to avert, to divert, to turn away from, or to reroute.

Using the image of "rerouting," let us compare the will to
a coachman and the emotions to four powerful horses. The
names of these horses are joy, hope, sorrow, and fear—the four
natural passions or emotions of the soul (A.3.16.2). The coachman's job is to steer these horses in the right direction: toward
God. But if the coachman lets go of the reins and loses control, the horses will run wild.

We all know by experience the havoc that ensues when we
let our emotions run wild. Conversely, when reason is in the
driver's seat and our emotions are directed toward doing God's
will, peace, order, and inner harmony will result. "When these
emotions go unbridled they are the source of all the vices and
imperfections, but when they are put in order and calmed they

give rise to all the virtues" (A.3.16.5). As we begin our consideration of the will and the passions of the soul (John's focus is on the passion of joy), there are a few basic aspects of John's teaching that we need to keep in mind.

First, John focuses on what he calls "active joy," that is, the happiness or satisfaction that we receive when we obtain an object that we have freely chosen to pursue. "We are speaking of active joy, which occurs when a person understands distinctly and clearly the object of its joy and has the power (*está en su mano*) either to rejoice or not" (A.3.17.1).

Está en su mano literally means "it is in your hand." In short, John is talking about what we choose to pursue. What we seek or don't seek is our choice; it is "in our hands," so to speak. Thus, John is not dealing with what we can call natural or spontaneous joy. For example, we do not choose to find joy in a beautiful sunset. We do not have any power over whether or not we are touched by a magnificent piece of music. We need to keep in mind that John is dealing with the joy of the will.

Second, the four passions are interrelated. Here, John paints a very homey picture of four brothers walking arm in arm, pulling one another in different directions. "These four passions are so interlinked and brotherly that where one goes actually the others go virtually" (A 3.16.5). Here John is saying that the four passions are interconnected emotional responses to what we seek in life. For example, if my greatest hope in life is to become the CEO of the company for which I work, I will be overjoyed if I obtain this position, dejected in sorrow if I am not promoted, and live in fear that my ambition will not be realized. In short, "Where your *treasure* is, there your *heart* will be also" (Mt 6:21).

Third, as we grow in charity, these passions do not decrease. Rather, they become more and more centered around doing the will of God, until they are "so ruled that a person rejoices only in what is purely for God's honor and glory, hopes for nothing else, feels sorrow only about matters pertaining to this, and fears only [not doing the will of] God" (A.3.16.2). Thus, for John, grace neither destroys nor represses nature—it perfects it.

For Reflection	We all know from experience the havoc and misery that ensue when our emotions are in the driver's seat. We know how difficult it is to keep a tight rein on them. In what areas of my life do my unbridled emotions wreak havoc? Conversely, at what moments have I experienced peace because I chose to do God's will in the face of strong emotions?

Joy in Temporal Goods

We can seek our joy in what John terms six categories of goods: temporal, natural, sensory, moral, supernatural, and spiritual (A.3.17.2). John's schema of treating each category is threefold: first, how we should direct our joy toward God by means of these objects; second, the harm that results if we fail to do so; and third, the benefits that are derived from rejoicing in them correctly.

TEMPORAL GOODS: DIRECTING OUR JOY TO GOD

There is a story of an old man who once asked a young lad what he was going to do when he grew up. The young boy said, "I'm going to go to college." "What then?" asked the old man. "Then, I'll get a good-paying job." "What then?" was the rejoinder. "Then, I'll get married and have a family." "What then?" "Then, when my children have all grown up, I'll retire and relax." "What then?" With this last question, the young boy paused and thought. After a moment he answered soberly. "Well, I guess then I will die." And the old man nodded his head and asked one more time, "What then?"

This story captures the essence of chapter 18 of book three of *The Ascent*, titled "Joy in temporal goods. How a person should direct it to God." In spite of the title, John never explicitly tells us how to direct our joy to God concerning temporal goods. Rather, he sets before us the chief danger of becoming absorbed in the pursuit of temporal goods, "the danger of forgetting God" (A.3.18.5).

"Forgetting God" is blindness. It is the inability to see temporal goods in the light of their ultimate end. Throughout this chapter, there is a refrain similar to the old man's question, "What then?" John asks if our relationship to "[temporal goods] is employed in the service of God" (A.3.18.3), or if it is "out of harmony with God" (A.3.18.6). In short, is our relationship to temporal goods in harmony with our eternal destiny?

Toward the end of chapter 18, John connects the "good times" of our lives with the danger of forgetfulness and the "bad times" of our lives with remembering our ultimate end. "Gladness is blinding to the heart and does not allow it to consider and ponder things while sadness makes people open their eyes" (A.3.18.5).

How true this is. When "all things are smiling and succeeding prosperously," we rarely think of our ultimate end (A.3.18.5). However, when some great sorrow comes into our lives, our eyes are opened, and we begin to ponder the meaning of our existence. Fostering the habit of looking at the goods of this world from the vantage point of death seems to be what John is recommending. By doing so, we both combat "the danger of forgetting God" and direct our joy in temporal things to God (A.3.18.5).

The temporal goods that John mentions, "riches, status, positions, . . . children, relatives, marriages," have one thing in common; they can become objects "claiming prestige (*pretensiones*)" (A.3.18.1). That is, we can make them ornaments of our egos. The human susceptibility to embroider one's ego with objects of the first series of temporal goods (riches, status, and positions) is self-evident. It is so unquestionable in John's mind that after citing several scriptural passages, he writes, "I do not want to add any more references here on so clear a matter, for I would never finish quoting Scripture" (A.3.18.2).

However, what about the second set of temporal goods (children, relatives, and marriages)? How are we to understand John's teaching regarding them? To do so, we need to remind ourselves that John is cautioning us against inordinate or disordered desires in relation to all temporal goods. For example, in regard to people having an inordinate desire for children, John writes, "It is also vain to desire children, as some do in upsetting (*hunden*) and troubling the whole world with their longing for them" (A.3.18.4). *Hunden* derived from *hundir* can mean "to submerge," "to immerse," "to put under water," "to sink," "to crush," or "to overwhelm."

How will the inordinate desire of the parent impact the life of his or her child? In what way will the child become overwhelmed by the need of his or her parent? For example, will the child become an extension of his or her parent's ego? Carl Jung's statement that "nothing exerts a stronger psychic effect upon children than the [unlived] life of the parents" may be turned into a question.[7] What influence is the unlived life of parents exerting upon their children? In what ways are the unfulfilled dreams and aspirations of parents visited upon their children? In what ways will the gifts, talents, or natural endowments of their children be exploited by their parents? We see a tragic example of this in Edith Wharton's novel *The House of Mirth*. Lily Bart, a young girl of great beauty, becomes the instrument used by her mother to regain the family's place in society.

Only one thought consoled her, and that was the contemplation of Lily's beauty. She studied it with a kind of passion, as though it were some weapon she slowly fashioned for her vengeance. It was the last asset in their fortunes, the nucleus around which their life was to be rebuilt. She watched it jealously, as though it were her own property and Lily its custodian; and she tried to instill into the latter a sense of the responsibility that such a charge involved. She followed in imagination the career of other beauties, pointing out to her daughter what might be achieved through such a gift, and dwelling on the awful warning of those who, in spite of it, had failed to get what they wanted.[8]

John might ask Lily's mother the following questions: Are the values that you are instilling in Lily for her ultimate good? Are they directed to her ultimate happiness? "As for children, there is no reason to rejoice in them because they are many, or rich, or endowed with natural talents and gifts, or because they are wealthy. One should rejoice in them if they are serving God" (A.3.18.4).

Next, John turns to intimacy in marriage. Here, John states that marriage can be the cause of a couple not centering their hearts on God but on one another (A.3.18.6). Again, John is saying that a good intimacy between two people can be at odds with the couple's ultimate good. This can happen, for example, when the intimacy between two people becomes inbred, what psychologist Erik Erikson calls a "pseudo-intimacy," or "an isolation *à deux*."[9]

An example of "an isolation *à deux*" can be found in Sheldon Vanauken's account of the early years of his marriage to his wife Jean. Besides romantic love, the Vanaukens shared a deep intellectual and aesthetic intimacy. At first glance, their marriage seemed idyllic. Rightly so, they did what was necessary to protect the bond between them. But as Vanauken points out, this bond that they referred to as "The Shining Barrier—the shield of our love" gradually began to isolate them from the world; it became "a walled garden" that protected them from "creeping separateness."[10]

> Creeping separateness and sharing were opposite sides of one coin. We rejected separate activities, whether bridge or shooting or sailing, because they would lead to creeping separateness; on the other hand, if one of us liked anything, the other, in the name of sharing, must learn to like it, too. It was now that we re-examined our doubts about children. If children could be raised by a nanny, we sharing them for a few hours each day, or even if we were farmers, children might be good. But in the pattern of modern life, where they became the centre for the woman, they were separating. We would have no children. Nor would we allow any career, unless we pursued it together, to become dominating. . . . How could one of us bear the death of the other? . . . So we completed the Shining Barrier: we would die together. If one were killed by sudden chance, the other would follow instantly. Or if one were mortally ill or when both of us became too old and frail to enjoy life, then we would go. We would take a plane up, up into the high pure sky, and put the nose down, thundering straight downwards, a bright arrow in the sunlight.[11]

Intimacy in marriage is a fragile reality that should be protected from the disintegrating forces of the world. For example, every couple knows that the demands of daily life can make time spent together virtually impossible. And unless a couple carves out time to be together, they can drift apart. The fear of drifting apart, or what Vanauken calls "creeping separateness," was the underlying motive to construct the "Shining Barrier." Unfortunately, this good motive became inordinate. The "Shining Barrier" barricaded the Vanaukens from life.

Vanauken presents us with an example of what can happen when something that is good takes over our lives. So many of our vices are our virtues that have gone to seed, or to use John's words, have become inordinate.

TEMPORAL GOODS: THE HARM CAUSED BY PLACING ONE'S JOY IN THEM

In one of the *Screwtape Letters*, Wormwood has become discouraged. He feels he is making meager progress with the soul he has been assigned to tempt. His uncle Screwtape offers Wormwood the following perspective:

> You will say that these are very small sins; and doubtless, like all young tempters, you are anxious to be able to report spectacular wickedness. But do remember, the only thing that matters is the extent to which you separate the man from the Enemy. It does not matter how small the sins are, provided that their cumulative effect is to edge the man away from the Light out into the Nothing. Murder is no better than cards if cards can do the trick. Indeed, the safest road to Hell is the gradual one—the gentle slope, soft underfoot, without sudden turnings, without milestones, without signposts.[12]

This passage contains the essence of John's teaching on the harm caused from joy in temporal goods. For John, like Lewis, the object that causes us harm is inconsequential, for "something very small can lead into great evils" (A.3.19.1). The great evil in question is the gradual edging of a soul "away from the Light out into the Nothing." Or as John puts it, it is "the privative harm . . . the withdrawal from God . . . that breeds every harm and evil in the soul" (A.3.19.1). For the remainder of chapter 19, John sets before us the "four degrees" of withdrawal from God.

The first degree of harm is identical to the "positive" harm of blindness that John dealt with in chapter 8 of book one of *The Ascent*. There, he wrote of the mind's judgment becoming "murky," "muddy," "hazy," and "clouded" (A.1.8.1). Here, John writes of the "blunting of the mind in relation to God . . . a dullness of mind and darkness of judgment in understanding truth and judging well of each thing as it is in itself" (A.3.19.3).

This blunting or dulling of the mind is the result of the soul's having become "surfeited (*empachara*) by engulfing itself in the joys of creatures" (A.3.19.3). *Empachara*, derived from *empachar*, means to be fed to satiety or to glut. Thus, the image behind John's first degree of harm is a person who has become groggy or drowsy after stuffing himself or herself with a big meal.

"The second degree of this privative harm issues from the first . . . [the soul] grew fat and . . . the will spread out and extended further to creatures" (A.3.19.5). This spreading out of the will is the result of the psychological dynamic of generalization by which a pleasurable, enjoyable, or gratifying experience in one area of life tends to generalize, extend, or spread to every area of life. For example, if we become attached to comfort in one area of life, we will gradually seek it in every other area of life. As St. Teresa observed, "A fault this body has is that the more comfort we try to give it the more needs it discovers. It's amazing how much comfort it wants" (W.11.2).

The third degree is a gradual shift of the soul's energy. Souls become "*sluggish* about matters pertaining to their salvation, they become more *alive and astute* in the things of the world" (A.3.19.7; italics added). In short, the soul becomes bored with God ("sluggish") and energized ("becomes more alive") in its pursuit of temporal goods.

The great danger of this shift is that the person can live with the illusion that nothing has changed. The illusion is sustained by the fact that for many years, "through mere formality, force, or habit," a person can continue to perform her or his spiritual exercises (A.3.19.6). However, over time, even these practices are gradually abandoned. When this happens, a rude awakening can occur, namely, that one has lost the desire and energy to do the will of God. The person can even feel, with a deep sense of despair, that what it has lost can never be recovered. F. Scott Fitzgerald recounts such a rude awakening in his autobiographical essay "The Crack-Up":

> There is another sort of blow that comes from within— that you don't feel until it's too late to do anything about it, until you realize with finality that in some regard you will never be as good a man again. This type of breakage happens almost without your knowing it but is realized suddenly indeed. . . . I began to realize that for two years my life had been drawing on resources that I did not possess, that I had been mortgaging myself physically and spiritually up to the hilt. . . . "*Ye are the salt of the earth. But if the salt hath lost its savour, wherewith shall it be salted?*"[13]

The fourth degree of harm is the ultimate outcome of a person who has sacrificed her or his life's blood to the pursuit of temporal goods. The tragic consequences of this harm are realized when these goods fail. In this regard, John puts before us a gruesome image; riches have become a pagan god who exacts human sacrifice.

> Included in this category of this last degree are all those miserable souls who . . . do not hesitate to sacrifice their lives when they observe that this god of theirs undergoes some temporal loss. They despair and commit suicide for wretched reasons, and demonstrate with their own hands the miserable reward that comes from such a god. And those whom he does not pursue right up to death, the ultimate injury, die from living in the affliction of anxieties and many other miseries. He does not permit gladness to enter their hearts or for any earthly good to bring them joy. Insofar as they are afflicted about money, they are always paying the tribute of their hearts to it. They cling to it unto their final calamity of just perdition, as the Wise man warns: "Riches are hoarded to the harm of their owner" [Eccl. 5:12]. (A.3.19.10)

Thus, John ends his consideration of the harm that we do to ourselves in the pursuit of temporal goods with a warning as compassionate as it is sobering. He sets before us the self-inflicted misery of our vain pursuits. A portrait of a "miserable soul" that has become addicted to a "miserable reward . . . clinging to its final calamity."

BENEFITS DERIVED THROUGH THE WITHDRAWAL OF JOY FROM TEMPORAL GOODS

Restlessness, St. Thomas Aquinas tells us, is one of the offspring or "daughters of covetousness."[14] All of us have made her acquaintance. How many restless nights have you tossed and turned in bed worrying about either obtaining or retaining something that you don't really need? How accurate is Dante's description of the burden of anxiety engendered by an inordinate desire for the goods of this world:

> It is the cause of evil, because it makes the possessor wakeful, timid, and hateful. How great the fear is that of a man who knows he carries riches about him, in journeying, in resting, not only when awake but when sleeping, not only that he will lose his property, but his very life for the sake of his property. Well do the miserable merchants know, who go about the world, that the leaves which the winds stir make them tremble when they are carrying their riches with them; and when they are without it, full of confidence, singing and talking they make their journey shorter.[15]

Dante captures the insidious nature of temporal goods. Once they are possessed, they can possess the possessor. The fear of being dispossessed fills every waking moment with anxious vigilance and keeps us wakeful, lest the thief break in and steal. How tragic that the soothing sound of rustling leaves outside one's bedroom window that should lull one to sleep keeps the rich man wakeful.

In Leo Tolstoy's story "The King and the Shirt," a king grew ill and could not sleep. No one knew what to do except one of the king's wise counselors. "If you can find a happy man, take his shirt, and put it on the king—and the king will be cured."[16] The king dispatched his servants to find such a man, but to no avail. One day, however, the king's son was passing by a poor little hovel and heard a voice come from inside: "Now, God be praised, I have finished my work, I have eaten my fill, and I can lie down and sleep! What more could I want?" The king's son rejoiced. At last, a truly happy man. But when he went into the hut to obtain the man's shirt, he discovered "the happy man was so poor that he had no shirt."[17] The juxtaposition of Dante's fearful rich man with Tolstoy's happy poor man symbolizes the essence of John's teaching of the fundamental benefit derived through withdrawing joy from temporal goods.

> Even if human beings do not free their hearts of joy in temporal goods for the sake of God and the demands of Christian perfection, they ought to do so because of the resulting temporal advantages, prescinding from the spiritual ones. . . . They acquire the virtue of liberality. . . . Moreover, they acquire liberty of spirit, clarity of reason, rest, tranquility, peaceful confidence in God. . . . They obtain more joy and recreation in creatures through the dispossession of them. They cannot rejoice in them if they behold them with possessiveness, for this is a care that, like a trap, holds the spirit to earth and does not allow wideness of heart. (A.3.20.2)

The "immediate objective" of liberality, writes St. Thomas Aquinas, is "the inner emotions" of joy and sorrow.[18] This is because the spiritual effect of liberality is being free from sorrow and acquiring the capacity for joy. "When someone lets something go, he liberates *it*, from his care and control."[19] The *it* that is liberated from care and control is not the object but the soul. Liberality releases the soul from being controlled by the need to control. And when a soul is released from the stranglehold of tight-fisted possessiveness by "open-handed liberality," to use Aristotle's phrase,[20] it can breathe freely, for it has gained a wideness of heart. It no longer has to hold its breath, lest someone snatch its possessions from its clenched fists.

The nonpossessive person can relax and discover more joy in life, for he or she has "obtain[ed] more joy and recreation *in creatures* through the dispossession of them" (A.3.20.2; italics added). Because the detached soul is able to let things just be, it is able to "delight in the substance" of things (A.3.20.2). It is only the nongrasping gaze that is able to see objects as they truly are. As Rainer Maria Rilke puts it, "Not till it is held in your renouncing is it truly there."[21]

For Reflection   Have I ever felt possessed by my possessions? When in my life have I experienced the relief that comes from letting go of an obsessive pursuit of a temporal good, be it a person, a career, or an object?

Joy in Natural Goods

⤜⤛

The vanity of willful joy in natural goods and the method of directing them to God (A.3.21)

Natural goods (beauty, grace, elegance, bodily constitution, etc.), like temporal goods, are gifts from God. However, they do us harm when we invest our self-worth in them. Natural goods are transitory by nature. In time, they will all abandon us. "All will grow old and pass away" (A.3.21.2). Our strength wanes, our health declines, our beauty fades, and our youth withers. The aging process is painful for all of us, but how much more miserable people become when they have invested their identity in natural goods. We have an example of this in Cash Bentley, the protagonist of John Cheever's story "O Youth and Beauty!" Everything that Cash Bentley did, how he dressed, walked, and talked, shouted a "quality of stubborn youthfulness."[22] He refused to admit that he was no longer a young man. His pretense was never more evident than at parties in the suburb of Shady Hill. It had become a ritual. When Trace Bearden would chide Cash about his age and thinning hair, the gauntlet was thrown down. Cash, who was an old college track star, would have to prove to everyone, especially himself, that he was still the man that he once was.

> The chiding was preliminary to moving the living-room furniture. Trace and Cash moved the tables and the chairs,

the sofas and the fire screen, the woodbox and the footstool. Then if the host had a revolver, he would be asked to produce it. Cash would take off his shoes and assume a starting crouch behind a sofa. Trace would fire the weapon out of an open window, and the hurdle race would begin. Over the sofa went Cash, over the tables, over the fire screen and the woodbox. It wasn't exactly a race, since Cash ran it alone. There was not a piece of furniture in Shady Hill that Cash could not take in stride. The race ended with cheers, and presently the party would break up.[23]

However, at one such party, when Cash had almost completed his hurdle race, he tripped over a piece of furniture and came crashing down to the floor like a ton of bricks. His head was cut, his left leg was broken, and his life was changed. His ability to run the hurdle race was what had preserved his illusion of youth. "In losing the hurdle race, he had lost the thing that preserved his equilibrium."[24] He had lost his mental balance, his poise, his temper, and his composure. His self-possession was as shattered as his leg. "He was rude to his friends when they stopped in for a drink. He was rude and gloomy when he and his wife Louise went out. When Louise asked him what was the matter, he only murmured, 'Nothing, nothing, nothing,' and poured himself some bourbon."[25]

Though his leg healed eventually, Cash was a changed man. Everything irritated him; everything reminded him of his mortality. One night, when the Rogers were throwing a party for the young people of the neighborhood, the music of the band drifted into the Bentleys' house. Cash went into the dark kitchen and drank. He was seized with bitter jealously. "Then jealousy seizes him—such savage and bitter jealously that he feels ill. He has been a young man. He has been a hero. He has been adored. . . . And now he stands in a dark kitchen, deprived of his athletic prowess, his impetuousness, his good looks—everything that means anything to him."[26]

The next evening Cash was restless. He went to the country club and drank. "He left the bar and banged into a table on his way through the lounge to the ballroom. He cut in on a young girl. He seized her too vehemently and jigged her off in an ancient two-step. She signaled openly for help to a boy in the stag line, and Cash was cut out. He walked angrily off the dance floor."[27]

The following evening, the Parminters invited Cash and Louise over for a drink. Cash went alone and became more depressed. On arriving home, he went upstairs to bed but quickly came down again.

> Louise heard him moving the living-room furniture around. Then he called to her, and when she went down, he was standing at the foot of the stairs in his stocking feet, holding the pistol out to her. She had never fired it before, and the directions he gave her were not much help.
>
> "Hurry up," he said, "I can't wait all night."
>
> He had forgotten to tell her about the safety, and when she pulled the trigger nothing happened.
>
> "It's that little lever," he said. "Press that little lever."
>
> Then in his impatience, he hurdled the sofa anyhow. The pistol went off and Louise got him in midair. She shot him dead.[28]

What killed Cash Bentley was his inability to accept that "all things will grow old and pass away like a garment, while God alone will remain immutable forever" [Ps. 102:26–27] (A.3.21.2). He could not accept that the natural goods with which he was endowed were mutable.

If Cash could have talked to John, John would have given him two pieces of advice. First, he would have told Cash that he had to stop running the hurdle race. "[You] must purge (*purgar*) and darken [your] will of this vain joy" (A 3.21.2). Every time Cash successfully completed the hurdle race, the applause of others not only reinforced his behavior but also helped him to maintain his illusion of youth. The only way Cash could purge (*purgar*), that is, purify, cleanse, or detox his will of the poisonous joy ingested into his soul by his display of "vain ostentation" was to stop the behavior that was feeding it (A.3.21.1).

The second piece of advice that John would have given Cash is to meditate on the transitoriness of life. "Spiritual persons, then, must purge and darken their will of this vain joy, and bear in mind (*advirtiendo*) the following: Beauty and all other natural endowments are but earth, arising from the earth and returning to it; grace and elegance are but the smoke and air of this earth, and should be considered and valued as such for the sake of avoiding a lapse into vanity. . . . As David affirms, all these things will grow old and pass away like a garment, while God alone will remain immutable forever [Ps. 102:26–27]" (A.3.21.2).

How different Cash's life would have been if he had meditated often and deeply upon this one line from Scripture? What if he had borne in mind that all things grow old and wear out like a garment? To bear in mind (*advirtiendo*) means to take notice of, to observe, and to be instructed by. If Cash had taken to heart the truth that the Psalmist lays before us, what a difference such an acknowledgment would have made in his life.

No longer would he have had to wear the heavy persona of stubborn youthfulness or worry about his performance in the next hurdle race. His morose rudeness and bitter jealousy would have dissolved, and he would not have had to engage in "inappropriate things" such as cutting in on a teenage girl at a dance (A.3.21.1). His equilibrium would have been restored.

THE HARM RESULTING FROM THE JOY OF THE WILL IN NATURAL GOODS

Not only does investing one's worth in natural goods inflict emotional misery, but it also causes spiritual harm, privative harm and positive harms.

The privative harm is a certain loss of soul: "Pure spirit is infallibly lost in this kind of joy" (A.3.22.2). We have an example of this in Edith Wharton's novel *The House of Mirth*. Lily Barth became an object because she invested her worth in the natural good of beauty. Because Lily "was brought up to be ornamental," she became a glittering object to decorate a man's ego.[29] In becoming an object of desire, Lily became a thing. The privative harm that an inordinate attachment to natural goods wreaks upon the soul is that it dehumanizes it.

Regarding positive harms, John writes that while there are many harms that result from inordinate joy in natural goods, "fornication is a particular evil that follows directly from [inordinate] joy in natural goods" (A.3.22.1). This statement would lead us to believe that John will be writing about the evils of sexual intercourse outside of marriage. However, he doesn't. Rather, John deals with the prelude to fornication, the dance of flirting and seduction.

To illustrate this, let us think of a young woman who becomes aware of her own beauty because she is being flattered by men. As she senses the effect that she is having on them, she becomes intoxicated. Realizing that men find her attractive and recognizing the power that lies in her beauty, she begins to flirt with them. This may have been what John had in mind when he wrote that inordinate joy in beauty is "inciting (*mueve*) the senses to . . . sensual delight (*deleite*), and lust (*lujuria*)" (A.3.22.2).

Mueve, derived from *mover*, means to move or to set in motion. *Deleite* and *lujuria* encompass everything from emotional delight to sexual pleasure. In short, she is moved or "turned on" because she realizes that she has the power to "turn on" men. However, she is blinded by the excitement of her inordinate joy. She does not see the seductive designs that may be concealed in flattery. "This joy induces flattery and vain praises involving deception" (A.3.22.2). Or as St. Thomas puts it, "The false praise of the flatterer softens the mind."[30] The dance of flirting and seduction is but one example of what is true in so many areas of life. Whenever we practice our arts on others, we become blind to the fact that others are practicing their arts upon us.

John is setting before us a reality that is true for any natural good in which we inordinately invest our joy, be it beauty, intelligence, or any other physical or mental endowment. If we want to be praised for some natural endowment, we do so at our own peril. As Cicero writes, "Flattery . . . can injure no one, except him who accepts it and is pleased with it. And so it happens that the man who flatters himself and is most highly pleased with himself, listens with the greatest eagerness to flatterers."[31]

The great desire to be flattered for possessing a natural good is expressive of the great damage done to a soul that is inordinately attached to it. "Since natural goods are more intimate to a person than temporal goods, joy in them produces its imprint more quickly and effectively and ravishes more forcibly" (A.3.22.2). In other words, when we relate to a good with possessiveness, the more interior it is, the more damage it does to the soul. As the Latin proverb has it, "*Corruptio optimi pessima*," or the corruption of the best produces the worst.

The Benefits Acquired from Not Rejoicing in Natural Goods

We experience the benefits of detachment from natural goods when there is a "withdrawal of the heart (*apartar su corazón*)" from them (A.3.23.1). Here, John is not talking about mere behavioral change but a radical transformation of the mind and affections (*corazón*) that results in a complete rerouting of one's value system.

Apartar can be translated as "to separate," "to remove," or "to turn away from." People who have turned their hearts away from investing their joy in natural goods are like someone who has taken an exit off a busy highway and travels down a peaceful country road. They have removed themselves from the fierce competition of the crowd that is forever jockeying for first place in the minds of others. In commenting upon the line in *The Spiritual Canticle* "I no longer tend the herd," John writes of the stress that a soul experiences when it follows the crowd. "She usually has desires to serve the appetites of others, which she does through ostentation, compliments, flattery, human respect, the effort to impress and please people by her actions, and many other useless things. In this fashion she strives to please people, employing for them all her care, desire, work and finally energy" (C.28.7).

Who of us doesn't know the careworn exhaustion that results from trying to impress or please others? How haggard we become when we sacrifice to the god of human approval all of our energy. How different our lives become when we no longer participate in the maddening crowd's ignoble strife. It "begets deep tranquility of soul" (A.3.23.3). This is one of the most notable benefits that John says results from withdrawing our hearts from joy in natural goods.

For Reflection   In what ways do I use my natural gifts to either impress or please others? What are the consequences of this behavior? Have I ever experienced the relief that is derived from letting go of the need to use my natural gifts to impress and please people?

Joy in Sensory Goods

How the will should be directed to God through the purgation of . . . joy in sensory goods (A.3.24)

I was once told about an astonishing level of chastity attained by someone. There was a man who, having looked on the body of a beautiful woman, at once gave praise to its Creator and after one look was stirred to love God and to weep copiously, so that it was marvelous how something that could have brought low one person managed to be the cause of a heavenly crown for another.[32]

This passage written by St. John Climacus reflects one of John's essential teachings on sensual, or sensory, goods (pleasure derived through the five exterior senses and the imagination), namely, that they are meant to be a means to lead us to God and become so when the will is purified and transformed. "When the will, in becoming aware of the delight afforded by an object of sight, hearing, or touch, does not stop with this joy but immediately elevates itself to God, being moved and strengthened for this by that delight, it is doing something very good. The will, *then*, does not have to avoid such experiences when they produce this devotion and prayer, but it can profit by them, and even ought to for the sake of so holy an exercise" (A.3.24.4; italics added).

But until then, the soul must mortify itself of such pleasures. "Yet anyone who does not feel this freedom of spirit in these objects and sensible delights, but finds that the will pauses in and feeds on them, suffers harm from them and ought to turn from their use" (A.3.24.6).

Let us take an example. As you are driving to work, you turn on the radio and are greeted by the beauty of Beethoven's "Moonlight Sonata." As you listen to the slow, haunting melody of the first movement, you begin to feel a sense of peace as an image of soft moonlight, reflected on a lake, arises in your mind. You are filled with a sense of God's gentle presence. However, halfway through the stormy final movement of the sonata, you are picturing yourself as the soloist playing at Carnegie Hall before an enraptured audience. All the people whom you want to impress are in the audience, especially those dolts in your hometown who believed you would never amount to anything. You feel not only a sense of pride but also the sweet joy of a vindictive triumph.

One moment the music is nourishing your soul; the next moment it is feeding your ego. The moment you become conscious that this shift has happened, John would recommend that you stop feeding your ego. In short, turn off the radio. "Whenever spiritual persons on hearing music . . . immediately at the first movement direct their thought and affections of their will to God . . . it is a sign that they are profiting by the senses and the sensory part is a help to the spirit. . . . Yet anyone who . . . finds that the will pauses in and feeds on them, suffers harm from them and ought to turn from their use" (A.3.24.5–6).

The spiritual harm of feeding our egotistical fantasies, as illustrated by our example of listening to music, is obvious for two reasons. First, the fantasies are blatantly narcissistic. Second, the harm manifests itself in the process of listening to the music. However, the spiritual harm that ensues from an inordinate attachment to sensory pleasure is not always immediately evident but can manifest itself over time. The specific sensual experience that John refers to in this regard is the "refreshment of the senses under the pretext (*pretexto*) of prayer." What these souls call prayer, John says is "recreation rather than prayer" (A.3.24.4).

To understand what John means by activities that refresh the senses under the pretext or guise of prayer, we must recall his teaching on discursive meditation and contemplative prayer. There are only two ways by which the soul can obtain knowledge in prayer. The soul can conceive it by means of discursive meditation or receive it by means of contemplation. If neither is happening, then the soul is not engaged in prayer. It is idle. "Were individuals not to have this knowledge [derived from discursive meditation] or attentiveness to God [in contemplative prayer] . . . they would have no activity whatsoever relative to God" (A.2.14.6).

How do we differentiate this "recreation" of the senses from contemplative prayer, since one can easily counterfeit the other? John's answer is to look at the effects outside of prayer. If one's "prayer" is sheer laziness, if it lacks the effort of attending to God's presence, then the will is weakened in regard to responding to God. It engenders a "weakness (*flaqueza*) . . . rather than the quickening (*avivar*) of their will and its surrender to God" (A.3.24.4). The will becomes sluggish in its response to doing God's will. However, if the will is exercised during prayer, it is strengthened. In consequence, the will is quickened; it is energized to do God's will. In short, by their fruits you will know them.

THE HARM INCURRED BY THE DESIRE FOR WILLFUL JOY IN SENSORY GOODS

A weakness or sluggishness of the will results in a soft lifestyle characterized by "lukewarmness and spiritual tedium" (A.3.25.1), a "spiritual torpor" that "extinguishes [the spirit's] strength and vigor" and results in an "unresponsiveness of conscience and spirit" (A.3.25.5–6). Souls addicted to sensory joys sink into a somnolent and dissipated lifestyle, which results in moral laxity and sensual indulgence. It is a lifestyle that avoids anything that is unpleasant or requires effort. Such people create their own misery, being battered about by impulse and appetite. "And it leaves the soul incapable of moral and spiritual blessings, as useless as a broken jar" (A.3.25.6).

THE SPIRITUAL AND TEMPORAL BENEFITS RESULTING FROM THE DENIAL OF JOY IN SENSORY GOODS

The benefits that result from mortifying our inordinate joy in sensory goods are chiefly the fruits of the virtue of temperance. First, when the clamor of our impulses and appetites is hushed, we "become recollected in God" (A.3.26.2). Or as St. Thomas puts it, "Tranquility of soul (*tranquillitas animi*), though a general feature of every virtue, is especially prominent in temperance."[33] The tranquility of temperance is the fruit of the healing of the division between mind and body that results in a "purgation of enjoyment" (A.3.26.5). This, in turn, enables the soul to experience "the serenity of habitual joy in God by means of His creatures and works" (A.3.26.6).

John compares this benefit to the integration or innocence of Adam and Eve. "In the state of innocence all that our first parents saw, spoke of, and ate in the garden of paradise served them for more abundant delight in contemplation, since the sensory part of their souls was truly subjected and ordered to reason. The person whose sense is purged of sensible objects and ordered to reason procures from the first movements the delight of savory contemplation and awareness of God" (A.3.26.5). To make an analogy based on human physiology, a soul purged of sensible objects is like a purged colon. An excessive buildup of mucus in the colon decreases its capacity to absorb vital nutrients from the blood system. As a result, a person eats more and more because his or her appetite is never satisfied. But when the colon is cleansed, its capacity to absorb nutrients increases, and appetite decreases because the body's hunger is satisfied.

Likewise, purified souls have an increased capacity to receive spiritual nourishment from sensual experiences. Because they have undergone a "purgation of enjoyment," they experience "abundant delight" and "the delight of savory contemplation and awareness of God" in creatures (A.3.26.5). The more our senses are purified, the more they become receptors of the spiritual dimension of creation. And when sense and spirit are nourished together, our soul's hunger is satisfied.

For Reflection | Do I have an inordinate attachment to a sensory good that dominates my life? Is there a sensory good (e.g., music, art, etc.) that nourishes my soul?

Joy in Moral Goods

In chapter 27, John gives examples of moral goods in which we can seek joy. Included in this category are "the exercise of any of the virtues; the practice of the works of mercy; the observance of God's law; [and] political prudence and all the practices of good manners" (A.3.27.1). From a natural viewpoint, the practice of moral goods is very rewarding. "They bring along with them peace, tranquility, a right and ordered use of reason, and actions resulting from mature deliberation. Humanly speaking, a person cannot have any nobler possession in this life" (A.3.27.2).

Though the possession of moral goods can make us noble, the question always remains, "What do we seek to gain by possessing them?" Do we seek "self-interest . . . with respect to pleasure, comfort, [and] praise," or do we seek to do the will of God (A.3.27.5)? Thus, as John begins his treatment of moral goods, he reminds us that moral goods, like all other categories of goods, are good in themselves but become detrimental to spiritual progress if our relationship to them is inordinate.

John is particularly concerned about someone who takes an inordinate pride in moral goods because the more spiritual the object that a person prides himself in, the deeper is the corruption of the soul. This is why John tells us, "Because this harm is spiritual it is particularly ruinous" (A.3.28.1).

SEVEN KINDS OF HARM THAT RESULT
FROM JOY OF THE WILL IN MORAL GOODS

Pride is the first harm that John considers. It is particularly ruinous to the soul because it renders it "*unable* to rejoice (*gozarse*) over one's works without esteeming them (*estimarlas*)" (A.3.28.2; italics added). *Gozar* means to enjoy, whereas *estimar* can be translated as to value, to make much of, or to form an opinion. Thus, prideful people are unable to enjoy what they possess because pride evaluates and esteems everything in relationship to the prestige that it confers. This evaluation is particularly ruinous to the soul because the basis of the soul's self-evaluation becomes dependent upon public recognition and the opinion of others.

This self-evaluation of these prideful persons breeds the second evil: "comparisons" with others, which makes them competitive for the limelight (A.3.28.3). In consequence, these souls "become angry and envious in noticing that others receive praise or accomplish more or have greater value than they themselves" (A.3.28.3). These souls try to simultaneously exalt themselves and tear others down by donning a "holier than thou" attitude. "Many today also [make comparisons in judging others] when they boast: 'I am not like so and so, nor do I do anything similar to what this or that one does'" (A.3.28.3).

This "I never" attitude is a means of calling attention to one's moral superiority. In his article "On Taking Scandal," Father Frederick Faber writes, "To give scandal is a great fault, but to take scandal is a greater fault. . . . They regard it as a sort of evidence of their own goodness, and their delicacy of conscience. . . . They think they suffer very much while they are taking scandal; whereas in truth they enjoy it amazingly. . . . It calls attention to the difference between him and themselves."[34]

As pride in moral goods takes root in the soul, the motivation for the soul to perform moral works becomes corrupted. This is the third harm. Since motivation is what moves the soul to act, it will only perform moral works if in doing so it obtains recognition from others. "Since they look for satisfaction in their works, they usually do not perform them unless they see that some gratification or praise will result from them" (A.3.28.4).

This desire for praise engenders the fourth harm: being attached to human respect (A.3.28.5). Attachment to what other people think of them is manifested in various ways. "Some want praise for their works; others, thanks; others talk about them and are pleased if this person or that or even the whole world knows about them; at times, they want their alms, or whatever they are doing, to pass through the hands of another that it may be better known; others desire all these things together" (A.3.28.5).

Over time, what these souls want becomes a need. They desperately need the approval, praise, and recognition of others. The result is self-inflicted misery. "There is so much misery among human beings as regard to this kind of harm" (A.3.28.5). To illustrate how pathological the need for recognition can become, John gives us the following example: "[Some] perpetuate their own name, lineage or nobility; or they even go to the extent of having their coat of arms or heraldry put in the church, as if they want to put themselves there as an image where all may bend the knee" (A.3.28.5). John's example is frightening. He suggests that our need for praise can become so megalomaniacal that we want to be worshipped in God's house.

The fifth harm is a consequence of what happens when people are motivated by satisfaction or gratification in their works. They "lose the spirit of perseverance" (A.3.28.7). This results in a lifestyle characterized by "starting and stopping without ever finishing anything" (A.3.29.2). They begin projects with great gusto, their minds being filled with grandiose fantasies, but they quickly peter out when they get down to the nitty-gritty work of actualizing their dreams. The wake of their lives is strewn with half-done projects. To work with these people is frustrating. They are very enthusiastic about any venture at the outset but never follow through on anything. They are unreliable. You can't count on them to do their part. What they do or don't do all depends upon their feelings.

The sixth harm is a distortion of judgment. "They are usually deluded by the thought that the exercises and works that give them satisfaction are better than those that do not" (A.3.28.8). Take, for example, a man who obtains great satisfaction from working in a soup kitchen. He is utterly convinced that his time spent in the soup kitchen is of greater worth in the eyes of God than spending time at home with his wife and his children because of the satisfaction he receives from his "ministry." He is so deluded by the satisfaction that he will not listen to what people are telling him, namely, that he is neglecting his family. This delusion results in the seventh harm: "[They] become incapable of taking counsel and receiving reasonable instructions about the works they ought to do" (A 3.28.9).

All seven harms distill into one evil: "Such people become very slack in charity toward God and neighbor, for the self-love contained in their works makes them grow cold in charity" (A.3.28.9). "The love of many will grow cold" (Mt 24:12). These words of Jesus are embedded in his apocalyptic discourse that contains frightening imagery of the stars falling from the sky and the moon and sun being darkened. Is there anything more chilling than the human heart that has grown cold in love?

The Benefits Derived from the Removal of Joy from Moral Goods

In Dickens's *Christmas Carol*, two gentlemen, in an effort to raise money for the poor, come to Scrooge's counting house in the hope of obtaining a donation. Scrooge is adamant in his refusal. He judges the poor to be lazy and regards himself as a realist and a shrewd man of business. In his arguments why he will not give anything to the poor, Scrooge alludes to Thomas Malthus's theory of population as a justification: "The poor should die and decrease the surplus population." This inhumane remark convinces the two gentlemen that continuing the conversation would be an exercise in futility, so they leave Scrooge's office. As Scrooge walks back to his desk, Dickens tells us that "Scrooge resumed his labours with an improved opinion of himself and in a more facetious temper than was usual with him." As Scrooge returns to his work in this happy state of mind, Dickens reveals to his readers what is happening to Scrooge's soul. "Meanwhile the fog and darkness thickened so, that people ran about with flaring links, proffering their services to go before horses in carriages and conduct them on their way. . . . The cold became intense. In the main street, at the corner of the court, some labourers were repairing the gas-pipes, and had lighted a great fire in a brazier, round which a party of ragged men and boys were gathered: warming their hands and winking their eyes before the blaze in rapture. The waterplug being left in solitude its overflowings sullenly congealed and turned to misanthropic ice."[35] What an image of Scrooge's heart! Sullen, frozen in hate, left in solitude, and outside the circle of humanity. Yet, his self-congratulatory feelings have blinded him to his spiritual condition. If feeling good about ourselves can make us blind to the spiritual damage we are doing to our souls in the wake of an act of callousness, how much more are we apt to be blinded by the feeling of pride subsequent to doing a good deed?

John begins chapter 29 by speaking of the "many temptations and deceits of the devil that are concealed *in the joy* of these good works" (A.3.29.1; italics added). In other words, the soul is blinded by its feelings of self-satisfaction in performing good deeds. The temptations and deceits are concealed or hidden "in the joy."

John singles out boasting as a behavior that deepens the blindness that is engendered by vain joy. "The vain joy itself is a deception, especially when there is some boastfulness of heart over one's works. As Jeremiah affirms: *Arrogantia tua decepit te* (Your arrogance has deceived you) [Jer. 49:16]. For what greater deception is there than boasting?" (A.3.29.1). John's insight is that the joy that is experienced as one is boasting makes a person oblivious or blind to reality. We have an example of this in the person of Frank Harris, a friend of Oscar Wilde. One night, at a social gathering, as Harris was monopolizing the conversation by his irritating habit of boasting of the important people whom he knew and the places to which he had been invited, Wilde, in a moment of exasperation, said, "Yes, dear Frank, we believe you have dined in every house in London—*once.*" Harris was blind to the fact that he was turning off the very people whom he was trying to impress.

The first benefit derived from the removal of joy from moral goods is that it frees the soul from such blindness; it becomes aware of the "hidden deceptiveness of this joy" and more attuned to how its behavior is affecting others (A.3.29.1).

The second benefit derived from being detached from the joy found in moral goods is that the soul acquires the strength of perseverance because its good deeds are not dependent upon feelings. This is in stark contrast to those who are attached to joy in moral goods: "Their work ends when the satisfaction ends" (A.3.29.2). John expresses this truth in Scholastic terminology. "The irascible and concupiscible appetites become so strong that [these souls] . . . become inconstant in their practice of good works" (A.3.29.2). Since John uses these terms several times in his writings, we'll now explore their meaning.

The Scholastics divided the emotions into concupiscible and irascible appetites. The concupiscible appetites regulate how we react to something that is good or evil. There are six concupiscible appetites: desire, love, joy, aversion, hate, and sorrow.[36]

Just as we desire what we love because it brings us joy, so we have an aversion to what we hate because it brings us sorrow. In short, the concupiscible appetites are our basic approach/avoidance reactions to objects. Desire is the movement toward the object of our love, and when we possess it, we feel joy. Conversely, we have an aversion toward what we find hateful and feel sorrow when we neither obtain what we love nor are able to avoid what we hate.

However, it is often difficult to obtain the good and avoid evil, either because of human weakness or external circumstances. At these times, other emotions come into play. These are called the irascible appetites, of which there are five: hope, despair, fear, daring, and anger.

When a good is hard to obtain, hope comes to our aid and buoys up our drooping spirits. Conversely, if we are overwhelmed by adversity, we can surrender to despair. And in the event that we cannot escape an evil, courage and fear are aroused. Courage energizes us to fight our foe; fear tends to make us cower before our foe.

The irascible appetites are grouped in pairs of opposites: hope with despair, fear with courage. Hope is desire in an arduous pursuit of a goal; despair is desire that has been defeated. Fear recoils in the face of danger, whereas courage strives to overcome the danger. Hope and courage are expressions of fight. Despair and fear are expressions of flight.

Finally, there is always an exception to the rule. Anger is the odd man out, the irascible appetite that stands alone and has no natural opposite. In Scholastic philosophy, ideally, the passion of anger is in the service of justice but can become vengeful and vindictive, concerned more with inflicting punishment upon the wrongdoer than with redressing a wrong.

Now that we have a sense of the nature of the concupiscible and irascible appetites, we can understand what John means when he says that in a soul attached to joy in moral goods, "the irascible and concupiscible appetites become so strong (*tan sobradas*) that they do not allow leeway (*lugar*) for the judgment of reason" (A.3.29.2). In short, these souls are completely ruled by their feelings.

Their emotions are *tan sobradas*, that is, so excessive, that there is no *lugar*, no place, no room within these souls that will listen to the voice of reason. All their decisions are based on pure emotionality. They live an exhausting life, being jerked about by their feelings.

The blessing that souls receive through the removal of joy from moral goods is a more peaceful and sane way of living. "They will act neither impetuously and hastily compelled by the irascible and concupiscible aspect of joy; nor presumptuously . . . nor incautiously" (A.3.29.4). The curse of those who have an inordinate attachment to joy in moral goods is that they live frenzied lives. They are driven by emotion; they act impetuously and incautiously, wreaking havoc in their own lives and those of others.

For
Reflection

Do I take pride in my virtues? Is it important that people regard me as virtuous? John writes that some people "want praise for their works; others, thanks; others talk about them and are pleased if this person or that or even the whole world knows about them" (A.3.28.5). Have I ever experienced the relief of not needing to be praised, thanked, or recognized for my good works?

Joy in Supernatural Goods

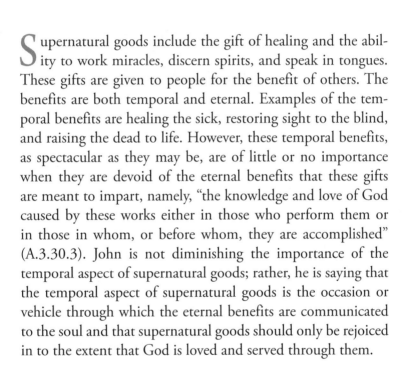

Supernatural goods include the gift of healing and the ability to work miracles, discern spirits, and speak in tongues. These gifts are given to people for the benefit of others. The benefits are both temporal and eternal. Examples of the temporal benefits are healing the sick, restoring sight to the blind, and raising the dead to life. However, these temporal benefits, as spectacular as they may be, are of little or no importance when they are devoid of the eternal benefits that these gifts are meant to impart, namely, "the knowledge and love of God caused by these works either in those who perform them or in those in whom, or before whom, they are accomplished" (A.3.30.3). John is not diminishing the importance of the temporal aspect of supernatural goods; rather, he is saying that the temporal aspect of supernatural goods is the occasion or vehicle through which the eternal benefits are communicated to the soul and that supernatural goods should only be rejoiced in to the extent that God is loved and served through them.

THE HARM RESULTING FROM REJOICING IN SUPERNATURAL GOODS

Those possessing a supernatural gift are vulnerable to pride. They can be tempted to use their gift for the sake of self-aggrandizement. John writes, "It is clear that in these cases those who were gifted were moved to perform their works at an inopportune time by some *imperfect* passion (*pasión*) that was clothed (*envuelta*) in *joy and esteem* for these works" (A.3.31.3; italics added).

To understand this passage, let us consider the following scenario. One evening, a charismatic prayer group leader, known to have the gift of discerning spirits, attends a function at his parish. Two admiring parishioners, seeking help in understanding a fellow parishioner's unusual behavior, approach him. He is so flattered by their confidence in his ability to read another person's heart that the imperfect passion (*pasión*) of pride is triggered within him. In consequence, he becomes enveloped or clothed (*envuelta*) in his feelings of self-importance and giftedness. Blinded by these feelings, he is moved to share his personal thoughts about the parishioner in such a way that he gives the impression that what he is saying is a result of insights given to him by God. However, no insight has been given to him by God. In truth, his remarks have arisen from feelings of self-importance in which he has become enveloped. This is an example of what John is saying. The man is "*moved* to perform [his] work at an inopportune time by some imperfect passion."

John teaches that a supernatural gift should never be used indiscriminately or inappropriately. Rather, its possessor needs to discern both when and how God wants it to be used. "Those, then, who have this supernatural gift should not desire or rejoice in its use, nor should they care about exercising it. God, who grants the grace supernaturally for the usefulness of the Church or its members, will also move the gifted supernaturally as to the manner and time in which they should use their gift" (A.3.31.7).

At the heart of John's teaching is a question. What moves a person to use his or her gifts, God or a self-serving motive?

This is an extremely important question in the spiritual life. Do we use our gifts, be they natural or supernatural, in the service of God or ourselves?

THE BENEFITS DERIVED FROM THE NEGATION OF JOY IN SUPERNATURAL GOODS

As Dante passes through the gate of purgatory proper, an angel carves on Dante's forehead seven *P*'s (for *peccata*, the Latin word for sin) that symbolize the seven capital sins that Dante will be purified of as he journeys up the mountain. As Dante is purified of each capital sin, an angel wipes a *P* off his forehead with its wing. After each successive *P* is removed, Dante's gait becomes more buoyant because he is less weighed down by sin. When all the *P*'s have been removed, Dante stands purified and transformed on top of Mount Purgatory. No longer being weighed down by sin, he is no longer held to earth. He and his guide Beatrice ascend upward to heaven praising God. (See *The Divine Comedy: Purgatorio*, canto 33, 141–145, and *Paradiso*, canto 1, 91–142.)

This image of Dante's purified soul, praising God as he ascends into heaven, symbolizes the twofold benefit of a soul that has become unburdened by detaching itself from seeking joy in the exercise of supernatural gifts. "The first refers to the praise and extolling of God; the second . . . the exaltation (*ensalzarse*) of the soul" (A.3.32.1).

The soul is exalted or uplifted when it "concentrates only on God [and is] centered on Him" rather than being weighed down by a preoccupation with self (A.3.32.2). Even though John is explicitly writing about those who are detached from supernatural goods, the relationship between focusing our minds on God and a corresponding lightness of being is a reality whenever we take our minds off ourselves and place them on our Supreme Good.

For Reflection	Is there a gift I have, supernatural or otherwise, that I am tempted to use inappropriately? Have I ever used my gift in a self-serving way? How did I feel afterward?

Joy in Spiritual Goods

⚜

What objects help and motivate you to live a deeper spiritual life? Are they statues, images, special places for prayer, or ceremonies? John's focus from chapters 35 through 45 is on the use of such objects. What is the purpose of these spiritual goods? How should they be used? When do they become obstacles to spiritual growth?

What we see in this final section of *The Ascent* is a principle we have seen throughout the work. All things are good and are meant to lead us to God but can hinder spiritual progress if we develop an inordinate relationship to them. This principle is especially instructive regarding spiritual goods because of the common assumption that if an object is explicitly religious (e.g., a statue of a saint, a rosary, etc.), it poses no potential spiritual harm. John says just the opposite. "Perhaps these images are *more dangerous*, for in saying 'they are holy objects' these persons become more assured and do not fear natural possessiveness and attachment. Spiritual persons are thus at times seriously deluded by thinking they are filled with devotion because of their satisfaction in the use of these holy objects" (A.3.38.1; italics added).

DOLL DRESSERS

Because of the delusion that holy objects can do no harm, people can become tragically ridiculous in their "devotion."

"They adorn statues with the jewelry conceited people in the course of time invent to satisfy themselves in their pastimes and vanities. . . . By this practice the authentic and sincere devotion of the soul . . . is reduced to little more than doll-dressing" (A.3.35.4).

The irony of these "doll dressers" may be illustrated by the following comic example. If you look at most Russian and Greek icons of the Blessed Virgin holding the child Jesus, you will see that one of Mary's hands is prayerfully pointing to Jesus. The gesture is symbolic of Mary's role in salvation. She leads us to her son. Her hand points to her son, to direct our gaze to him. Now think of a person who owns such an icon and spends all of his or her time beautifying Mary's hand by painting the nails and adorning them with decals and imitation jewels. The person stands back to admire the beauty of the hand and then invites friends in for coffee and a showing.

This example, though meant to be comical, has a serious subscript. It illustrates John's teaching of the harm that such behavior causes, which "is by no means slight" (A.3.35.8), for "the delight they find in these ornate paintings withdraws their attention from the living person presented" (A.3.38.2). "The more they are attached with a possessive spirit to the image or motive, the less their prayer and devotion ascend to God" (A.3.35.6). In consequence, "these means which should be an aid in one's flight to God . . . [are now] a hindrance" (A.3.35.6).

INTERIOR DECORATORS

"Some individuals never grow tired of adding images of one kind or another to their oratories, or of taking delight in the arrangement and adornment of these images so the place of prayer will appear well decorated and attractive" (A.3.38.2).

The devotion of these interior decorators, like the doll dressers, is harmed by their attention to the décor of their oratories. The interior decorators that John is describing are also "collectors," who scurry about acquiring one object after another. If John lived in our day, he may have identified such "interior decorators" as pious individuals who spend an inordinate amount of time, energy, and money searching out religious items in antique shops, yard sales, and church bazaars.

AESTHETICS

John's teaching that having an inordinate attachment to the outward appearance of religious objects, whether statues, rosaries, or the décor of oratories, should not lead us to conclude that he is indifferent to the importance of aesthetics in religious art. For John also says that some statues are carved "so inexpertly that the finished statue *subtracts from devotion*" (A.3.38.2; italics added). John feels so strongly about this that he recommends that these inept artists "should be forbidden to continue their craft" (A.3.38.2). It is the work of such artists as these that gives credence to St. Thérèse's belief that if the saints came back to earth, most of them would not recognize themselves. In short, just as an inordinate attachment to the aesthetics of a statue can hinder devotion, so too can a crude representation of a saint.

Even though possessing a good aesthetic sense is a gift from God, it can prove to be problematic if a person becomes attached to his or her taste in religious art. "They will be rendered incapable of praying everywhere. They will be able to pray only in those places *suited to their taste*, and thus be frequently wanting in prayer" (A.3.41.1; italics added).

John is against not the use of images and sacramentals but their abuse and our attachment to them. He draws our attention to their importance in the spiritual life. "The Church established the use of images for two principal reasons: the reverence given to the saints through them; and both the motivation of the will and the awakening of devotion to the saints by their means. Insofar as they serve this purpose their use is profitable and necessary" (A.3.35.3).

In short, images of saints are meant to strengthen us in doing God's will. They are meant to be windows through which we peer to see that which is holy. Unfortunately, some people become fixated on the window dressing, which "is a total obstacle to authentic spirituality" (A.3.35.3).

CEREMONIES

Freud said there is a great resemblance between religious ceremonies and the ritualistic behaviors of obsessive-compulsives. Both perform their rites scrupulously. Both believe that no detail can be added or omitted. Both are convinced that the efficacy of the ritual is determined by how it is performed.

Even though John would have disagreed with Freud's belief that religion is the universal obsessional neurosis of the human race, I think he would have been very interested in what Freud had to say on the subject. I say this because Freud's connection between obsessive-compulsive behavior and the way that some people perform their religious ceremonies corresponds to John's own observations. John writes:

> I want to speak only of those ceremonies that are used by many today with indiscreet devotion (*con devoción indiscreta*) . . . of those who attribute so much efficacy to methods of carrying out their devotions and prayers and so trust in them that they believe that if one point is missing or certain

limits have been exceeded their prayer will be profitless and go unanswered. As a result they put more trust in these methods than they do in the living prayer. . . . They demand that the Mass be said with a certain number of candles, no more nor less; or that it be celebrated at a particular hour, no sooner or later; or that it be said after a certain day, not before, or that the prayers and stations be a particular number and kind and that they be recited at certain times and with certain ceremonies, and neither before nor after, nor in any other way; and that the person performing the ceremonies have certain endowments and characteristics. (A.3.43.2)

The people whom John is describing in the above passage run the gamut from full-blown obsessive-compulsives to all of us who insist on having things "just so." Are not many of us "just so" people when it comes to liturgy? Don't we all have our personal rubrics about how we feel the liturgy should be performed?

This is not to say that there is anything wrong with having preferences regarding how the Eucharist is celebrated. That is just a part of being human. Some people prefer a more contemplative celebration of the Eucharist, others a more charismatic one. Some of us favor a more "conservative" Mass, others a more "liberal" one. What John is concerned about is how attached we are to our preferences. Do we worship "with indiscreet devotion" (*con devoción indiscreta*)?

Indiscreta can simply mean being indiscreet but can also mean being intrusive or pushy. John may not have had these various meanings of *indiscreta* in mind when he wrote the above passage; nevertheless, he is describing people who insist on their own way, those who often push their own agenda. This is where the problem lies: being attached to one's own way. The privative harm of an inordinate attachment to having the liturgy tailored to one's taste is that one becomes so obsessed with the externals of the ceremony that one's mind is taken off God.

How can one detach oneself from an inordinate attachment to having the Eucharist celebrated in a precise manner? What can one do to avoid being preoccupied with how the Mass is being celebrated? J. R. R. Tolkien, a devout Roman Catholic who had a great love for the Eucharist, once gave his youngest son Michael the following advice in this regard:

> Also I can recommend this as an exercise (alas! Only too easy to find opportunity for): make your Communion in circumstances that affront your taste. Choose a snuffling or gabbling priest or a proud and vulgar friar; and a church full of the usual bourgeois crowd, ill-behaved children— from those who yell to those products of Catholic schools who the moment the tabernacle is opened sit back and yawn—open necked and dirty youth. Go to Communion *with* them (and pray for them). It will be just the same (or better than that) as a Mass said beautifully by a visibly holy man, and shared by a few devout and decorous people.[37]

This is advice that John could have given to a directee, for it is an example of his ascetical principle laid down in chapter 13 of book one of *The Ascent*: be inclined toward the opposite. Tolkien is advising his son to freely choose to put himself in a position that affronts his sensibilities, for the sake of becoming free of them.

MIRACULOUS STATUES

There are several miraculous "Weeping Madonna" statues to which one can make a pilgrimage (e.g., Rockingham, Australia; Syracuse, Italy; Medford, Massachusetts; and Toronto,

Canada, to name a few). What advice would John give to people who have booked a reservation on an excursion to one of these sites?

First, John would point out that there is nothing magical about a specific statue, and it would be foolish for pilgrims to "think that God will answer them more readily through it . . . for God looks only on the faith and purity of the prayerful heart" (A.3.36.1). Second, he would make it clear that even "if God sometimes bestows more favors through one statue than through another, He does not do so because of its greater ability to produce the effect . . . but because the devotion of individuals is awakened more by means of one statue than the other. Were people to have equal devotion in the presence of both . . . God would grant them the same favors" (A.3.36.1).

In short, John would try to make these people understand that the most important part of the pilgrimage is neither praying before a statue nor having God grant their petitions but an increase of devotion.

John might ask these people to reflect upon the primary purpose of the pilgrimage. Is it spiritual or recreational? "For many go on pilgrimage more for the sake of recreation than devotion" (A 3.36.3). Or as the *Imitation of Christ* has it, "They who undertake many pilgrimages seldom become holy."[38]

John would also advise these people that any future pilgrimage be done alone and that one go to a place that is off the beaten track. "Our Lord frequently bestows these favors by means of images situated in remote and solitary places. The reason for this is that the effort required in journeying to these places makes the affection increase and the act of prayer more intense. . . . A person may also withdraw from people and noise to pray. Whoever makes a pilgrimage does well to make it alone. . . . I would never advise going along with a large crowd, because one ordinarily returns more distracted than before" (A.3.36.3).

I suspect that if people followed John's guidelines for making a pilgrimage, many tour companies that conduct pilgrimages to holy shrines, replete with side trips to "points of interests" and ample time allotted for shopping sprees, would go out of business.

PLACES TO PRAY

People who have an inordinate attachment to particular places "will be able to pray only in those places suited to their taste, and thus be frequently wanting in prayer" (A.3.41.1). However, John also says that there are certain places that are more conducive to prayer than others. He mentions three types of places "by which God . . . moves the will" (A.3.42.1).

The first includes "sites that have pleasant variations in the arrangement of the land and trees and provide solitary quietude, all of which awakens devotion" (A.3.42.1). In short, a pastoral setting far from the madding crowd can be conducive to prayer. However, the beauty of God's creation can also be an obstacle to prayer. This happens when we are merely "looking for delight . . . from a particular site and searching for sensory recreation" (A.3.42.2).

This statement challenges a very common assumption, namely, that an experience of nature is a spiritual experience. Yes, it can be an emotionally uplifting experience, but does it bring one closer to God? Does it strengthen the soul to do God's will? If what we are seeking in nature is a spiritual experience, then John would ask, "How is this different from a beginner who seeks consolation in prayer?" John would answer, "There isn't any difference."

Yet, John teaches that a beautiful setting can be an aid to prayer, provided it remains a vehicle for prayer and not a resting place. "It is advantageous to use these places if one immediately directs the will to God in forgetfulness of the place itself, since one should not be detained by the means and motive more than necessary to attain the end" (A.3.42.1).

The second type of place in which God often moves our will to devotion is a place in which we have so experienced the presence of God that we "have a natural inclination toward that place and sometimes experience intense desires and longings to return there" (A.3.42.3). Should a person return to such a place? That depends upon the person's motive.

The motive for some people returning to a place is emotional rather than spiritual. They return hoping to recapture a certain feeling. This motive becomes evident in their disappointment when they do not recapture the desired experience. "But on returning, that person discovers that the place is not what it was before because these favors do not lie within one's own power" (A.3.42.3). Since seeking an emotional experience is an attachment to consolation, John would advise these people to carefully reflect upon their motive for returning to these places.

Conversely, John says it "is good sometimes to return there for prayer, provided one's soul is divested of the desire for spiritual possessions" (A.3.42.3). And the good that is engendered in these souls is an increase of praise, thanksgiving, and devotion to God (A.3.42.3). What we see here is a principle of John's teaching that runs throughout *The Ascent*, namely, it is not the object that is in question but the soul's relationship to the object.

The third kind of place that John mentions is one "in which *God chooses* to be invoked and worshipped" (A.3.42.5; italics added). Mount Sinai, where God appeared to Moses, is an example of such a place. Such places are "more appropriate places for our prayers" because, in the course of salvation history, these are the places where God has chosen to manifest himself in special ways (A.3.42.6). "God alone knows why He chooses one place in which to receive praise more than another. What we should know is that He does all for our own benefit" (A.3.42.6.).

What is the benefit? John does not say. But perhaps it is to remind us of a truth that he has set before us many times in *The Ascent*, namely, that we are not in control of when and where God reveals himself to us.

PROVOCATIVE GOODS

The second category of spiritual goods that John mentions is called provocative (*provocativos*) goods, derived from *provocar*, meaning to rouse, to excite, or to move. They are goods "that arouse or persuade one to serve God" (A.3.45.1). John discusses only one kind of provocative good: preaching "with reference to the preacher himself and with reference to his hearers" (A.3.45.1). In short, John discusses how we should speak and how we should listen.

Those Who Speak

In Thomas Hardy's poem "In Church" we have an image of a preacher puffed up by pride after his performance, who "vainly rejoices" and is intoxicated by his power to "arouse" others, not for God's service but for his own glory (A.3.45.1).

> "And now to God the Father," he ends,
> And his voice thrills up to the topmost tiles:
> Each listener chokes as he bows and bends,

> And emotion pervades the crowded aisles.
> Then the preacher glides to the vestry-door,
> And shuts it, and thinks he is seen no more.
> The door swings softly ajar meanwhile,
> And a pupil of his in the Bible class,
> Who adores him as one without gloss or guile,
> Sees her idol stand with a satisfied smile
> And re-enact at the vestry glass
> Each pulpit gesture in deft dumb-show
> That had moved the congregation so.[39]

The clergyman in Hardy's poem could have benefited from St. Gregory the Great's warning that preachers should be aware of the great danger of "developing tumors of pride" which happens when "the mind of the speaker is exalted by joy . . . over his performance."[40] This is a great temptation of those who preach. As T. S. Eliot put in the mouth of Thomas Becket, "Servant of God has chance of greater sin. For those who serve the greater cause may make the cause serve them."[41]

Thus, in the last chapter of *The Ascent*, John's focus is on an inherent danger of his own vocation as a preacher. It is almost as if John were saying to himself and to his fellow friars, "Before you preach to others, look to your own house. You have been entrusted with an important task, so preach in such a way as to 'arouse or persuade [others] to serve God,' not to feed your ego" (A.3.45.1).

> As for the preacher, in order to benefit the people and avoid the impediment of vain joy and presumption, he should keep in mind that preaching is more a spiritual practice than a vocal one. For although it is practiced through

exterior words, it has no force or efficacy save from the interior spirit. No matter how lofty the doctrine preached, or polished the rhetoric, or sublime the style in which the preaching is clothed, the profit does not ordinarily increase because of these means in themselves; it comes from the spirit. . . . Although it is true that good style, gestures, sublime doctrine, and well-chosen words are more moving and productive of effect when accompanied by this good spirit, yet without it the sermon imparts little or no devotion to the will." (A.3.45.2, 4)

In this passage, John is underlining the primacy of the spiritual dimension of preaching. However, he does not scorn the human dimension. While the content (doctrine), style, and rhetoric of a homily are not its most important aspects, John does not minimize them. He simply says they are insufficient of themselves. Let us explore what John says regarding both the spiritual and human aspects of preaching.

The Life of the Preacher

Cardinal John Henry Newman, whose favorite composer was Beethoven, chose for his motto words written on the manuscript of Beethoven's composition, the *Missa Solemnis: Cor Ad Cor Loquitur* (Heart Speaks to Heart). These words express a deep spiritual truth, namely, that the deep truths of life are communicated on the level of the heart. Just as countless people who cannot read a note of music have been deeply moved by Beethoven's *Missa Solemnis*, so too is God's truth communicated in mysterious ways, one of which is true holiness.

True holiness is attractive and has the power to touch the human heart. Cardinal Newman, in his sermon "Personal Influence: The Means of Propagating the Truth," writes of this vital dimension of the preacher: "Men persuade themselves, with little difficulty, to scoff at principles, to ridicule books, to make sport of the names of good men; but they cannot bear their presence: it is holiness embodied in personal form, which they cannot steadily confront. . . . The attraction, exerted by unconscious holiness, is of an urgent and irresistible nature; it persuades the weak, the timid, the wavering and the inquiring; it draws forth the affection and loyalty of all who are in a measure likeminded; and over the thoughtless . . . multitude it exercises a sovereign compulsory sway."[42]

Goodness has an uncanny appeal; holiness that is mirrored in a person's life exerts an attraction over the human heart. This is the spiritual aspect of preaching of which John writes. "The better the life of the preacher the more abundant the fruit, no matter how lowly his style, poor his rhetoric, and plain the doctrine. For the living spirit enkindles fire. But when this spirit is wanting the gain is small, however sublime the style and doctrine" (A.3.45.4).

If the preacher is rooted in God's indwelling presence, then his words bear fruit in the lives of others. As St. Teresa writes, when a soul's active works arise from a deep "interior root, they become lovely and very fragrant flowers. For they proceed from the tree of God's love . . . [and] the fragrance from these flowers spreads to the benefit of many. It is a fragrance that lasts, not passing quickly, but having great effect" (SS.257).

Teresa is talking not merely about the power of good example but also about an aspect of divine grace. When we are touched by the speech of a holy person, we are being touched by the presence of God, for "it comes from the spirit" (A.3.45.2).

There is much to ponder here. Our fidelity in doing God's will is not only for our own sanctification but also for the sanctification of others. The more we are united to God, the more we will touch the lives of others.

Preparation

Though John emphasizes the sanctity of the preacher, he does not neglect the importance of preparation. "For the one who teaches, the profit is usually commensurate with his preparation. For this reason it is commonly said that as the master, so usually is the disciple" (A.3.45.3). In short, we cannot nourish others unless we take time to be fed.

First, the preacher's soul must be fed by God in prayer. As St. Augustine writes regarding the preacher, "Let him be a pray-er before being a speaker. At the very moment he steps up to speak, before he opens his mouth and says a word, let him lift up his thirsty soul to God, begging that it may belch forth what it has quaffed, or pour out what he has filled it with."[43]

Second, the preacher's mind must be fed if he is to impart truth. If a preacher is remiss in his duty to prepare his homilies, his congregation will be malnourished. Parishioners recognize when preparation has gone into a homily, and when the preacher is "winging it." In many parishes, when parishioners see Father Nonpreparatus walk down the middle aisle at the beginning of Mass, everyone groans. They know that their eyes will glaze over, and their heads will begin to nod as Father N. rambles and drones on about whatever thoughts just happen to be floating through his mind at the moment.

Father Nonpreparatus may not be a dynamic preacher, but this does not exempt him from his duty to prepare his homilies. Even the dullest preacher can seek out illustrations and stories that can enrich his sermons. We all know from experience that a well-chosen image or story has the power to imbue old truths with new life. They can "lift up and restore even those things that have fallen into ruin" (A.3.45.5).

To hunt down the right illustration for a sermon takes time and energy. It is a tedious act of love. But if preachers practice this form of love, then "better [is] the life of the preacher [and therefore] the more abundant the fruit" (A.3.45.4).

Being constant in doing one's duty is an essential ascetical practice. Being consistent in doing the unglamorous tasks of the daily round is the desert road. It is the insufferable barren track of life and the slow and steady ascent up Mount Carmel.

Those Who Listen

As John concludes his comments on those who stand in the pulpit, he turns toward those who sit in the pews, for a "two-fold preparation is required . . . that of the preacher and that of his hearers" (A.3.45.3). And here he sets before us the question, "When we listen to a sermon, what do we hope to gain?" Are we willing to change our lives as a result of the truth that we hear, or do we simply want to be entertained? As John puts it, "The sensory adherence to the gratification provided by the doctrine hinders any effect the doctrine may have on the spirit, and people are left only with esteem for the mode and the accidents of the sermon. They praise the preacher and listen to him for these reasons *more than* for the motivation they receive to amend their lives" (A.3.45.5; italics added).

These words reflect our ambivalence to the truth of the Gospel. They are similar to what Freud once said regarding why people enter therapy. He said that people come to therapy for two reasons: to be healed and to avoid being healed. All of us want to change our lives, but we are comfortable with the familiar. In a sermon, we want to hear a truth that will make us better people, yet our complacency hopes that the preacher will confirm us in the status quo. As usual, John offers us no suggestions on what we should do to prepare ourselves to listen to God's word. Yet, we will find no better practice than the one contained in his saying, "The Father spoke one Word, which was His Son, and this Word He speaks always in eternal silence, and in silence must it be heard by the soul" (SLL.100). Just as St. Augustine exhorted the preacher to "be a pray-er before being a speaker," so too, it would behoove us to be pray-ers before we are listeners.

For Reflection

Have my aesthetic taste and preferences regarding religious objects, ceremonies, and places to worship begun to limit my ability to focus my mind on God? In short, have they become a distraction to real prayer?

For all of us, as it is for the preacher, a central issue in the spiritual life is preparing for and fulfilling our daily duties. In this regard, each of us should ask ourselves two basic questions: Do I invest the necessary time and energy that my duties require, or do I expend the minimal time and energy in every task? What are the consequences of this choice?

CONCLUSION

There are two similarities between *The Ascent* and Bach's *Art of Fugue*. First, they both end abruptly. Bach breaks off in midphrase, and John ends in midsentence. In both incidences, we don't know why. Second, both are explorations of a single theme. Just as "the governing idea of [*The Art of Fugue*] is an exploration of the depth of the contrapuntal possibilities inherent in a single musical subject," so *The Ascent* is a series of variations on a single theme: all things are good and are meant to be means that will lead us to God.[44] However, they can become obstacles if we choose to take up a possessive relationship to them. John puts before us both the misery that comes from a possessive heart and the joy that God grants to a soul that loves freely.

Notes

PREFACE

1. Encyclical *Novo millennio ineunte* ("At the Beginning of the New Millennium"), January 6, 2001.
2. *The Interior Castle*, 5.1.2.
3. Letter n. 7, to the Carmelite nuns at Beas de Segura.
4. *The Ascent of Mount Carmel*, Prologue, n. 8.
5. T. S. Eliot, "The Dry Salvages," in the *Four Quartets* (New York: Harcourt, Brace & Jovanovich, 1971).

COMING TO TERMS

1. John deals with this in book II of *The Dark Night of the Soul*.
2. T. S. Eliot, *Four Quartets* (New York: Harcourt, Brace & Jovanovich, 1971), 58.

BOOK ONE

Appetite and Appetites

1. William F. Lynch, *Images of Hope* (New York: Mentor-Omega Books, 1965), 90–109.
2. Dante, *Inferno*, trans. John Ciardi (New York: New American Library, 1954), 45.

Harms

3. Charles Dickens, *A Christmas Carol and Other Christmas Stories* (New York: Signet Classics, 1984), 73.
4. Leo Tolstoy, *Anna Karenina*, trans. Constance Garnett (Cleveland: Fine Edition Press, 1946), 529.
5. Ibid., 544.
6. Eliot, *Four Quartets*, 17.

7. Ray Bradbury, *Fahrenheit 451* (New York: Ballantine Books, 1987), 54.

8. Fyodor Dostoevsky, *Crime and Punishment*, trans. Constance Garnett (New York: Bantam, 1987), 54.

9. Karen Horney, *Neurosis and Human Growth* (New York: Norton, 1950), 120.

10. George Eliot, *The Lifted Veil, Brother Jacob* (Oxford: Oxford University Press, 1999), 20–21.

11. William Shakespeare, *Complete Sonnets* (New York: Dove, 1991), 56.

12. St. Augustine, "The Christian Combat," in *The Writings of St. Augustine*, trans. John J. Gavigan, O.S.A., vol. 4 (New York: Fathers of the Church, 1947), 324.

13. Oscar Wilde, *The Picture of Dorian Gray* (New York: Bantam, 1982), 80–81.

14. F. Scott Fitzgerald, "Babylon Revisited," in *The Stories of F. Scott Fitzgerald* (New York: Macmillan, 1951), 389.

Threshold of Consent

15. Dante, *The Purgatorio*, trans. John Ciardi (New York: New American Library, 1961).

Counsel One: Growing in Habitual Desire

16. Pierre Descouvemont, *Thérèse of Lisieux and Marie of the Trinity*, trans. Alexander Plettenberg-Serban (New York: Alba House, 1993), 84–85.

17. Pope John XXIII, *Journal of a Soul*, trans. Dorothy White (New York: McGraw-Hill, 1965), 106–7.

18. St. Francis de Sales, *Introduction to the Devout Life*, trans. Michael Day (Wheathampstead, UK: Anthony Clarke, 1990), 11.

19. John Cassian, *The Institutes*, trans. Boniface Ramsey, O.S.B. (New York: Newman, 2000), 119.

20. St. Thomas Aquinas, *Summa Theologica*, II, II, Q. 47. a. 8.

21. St. Augustine, *The Confessions*, trans. Maria Boulding, O.S.B. (Hyde Park, NY: New City Press, 1997), 46.

Counsel Two: Renouncing Sensory Satisfaction

22. John Cassian, "Conferences," in *The Nicene and Post-Nicene Fathers*, trans. Edgar Gibson (Grand Rapids, MI: Eerdmans, 1964), 540.

23. St. Francis de Sales, *Introduction to the Devout Life*, trans. Michael Day (Wheathampstead, UK: Anthony Clarke, 1990), 174.

24. See St. Thomas Aquinas, *Summa Theologica*, II, II, Q. 168, a. 2.

25. Ibid., II, II, Q. 168, a. 2. reply.

26. Ibid., II, II, Q.168, a. 3.

27. John Cassian, *Conferences*, trans. Colin Luibheid (New York: Paulist Press, 1985), 76.

28. Mortimer J. Adler, *Six Great Ideas* (New York: Macmillan, 1981), 128.

29. Albert Ellis and Robert A. Harper, *A New Guide to Rational Living* (North Hollywood, CA: Wilshire Book Company, 1975), 158.

Counsel Three: Having Contempt for Self

30. St. Augustine, *The Confessions*, trans. Maria Boulding, O.S.B. (Hyde Park, NY: New City Press, 1997), 41–66.

31. St. Thomas Aquinas, *Summa Theologica* I, II, Q. 77, a. 5; italics added.

Counsel Four: To Have All, Renounce All

32. Christopher O'Mahony, trans. and ed., *St. Thérèse of Lisieux: By Those Who Knew Her* (Dublin: Veritas, 1975), 125.

The Fatal Pause

33. Flannery O'Connor, *Mystery and Manners: Occasional Prose* (New York: Farrar, Straus and Giroux, 1969), 118.

34. Anton Chekhov, "At the Mill," in *The Portable Chekhov*, trans. Avrahm Yarmolinsky (New York: Viking Press, 1947), 83.

35. Ibid., 85.

BOOK TWO

The Passive Night of Sense

1. C. S. Lewis, *The Screwtape Letters* (New York: Macmillan, 1961), 38–39.

Like Trying to Explain Color to a Blind Person

2. Thomas Green, *Darkness in the Marketplace* (Notre Dame, IN: Ave Maria Press, 1981), 94.

Love Is Not Blind; It Gives Sight

3. St. Thomas Aquinas, *The Sentences*, III, 35, 1, 2.

Just Talking

4. Anton Chekhov, *The Major Plays*, trans. Ann Dunnigan (New York: Signet Classics, 1964), xi.

BOOK THREE

The Hair Trigger of Memory

1. John Climacus, *The Ladder of Divine Ascent*, trans. Colin Luibheid and Norman Russell (New York: Paulist Press, 1982), 148.

2. Brother Lawrence of the Resurrection, *The Practice of the Presence of God*, trans. Salvatore Sciurba, O.C.D. (Washington, DC: ICS Publications, 1994), 93.

The Stomach of the Mind

3. Dante, *Inferno*, trans. John Ciardi (New York: New American Library, 1954), 277.

4. St. Augustine, *The Confessions*, trans. Maria Boulding, O.S.B. (Hyde Park, NY: New City Press, 1997), 193.

5. St. Augustine, *Letters*, trans. Wilfred Parsons, S.N.D., vol. 1 (New York: Fathers of the Church, 1951), 171.

Tranquility of Soul

6. St. Augustine, *The City of God*, trans. Henry Bettenson (New York: Penguin, 1980), 870.

Joy in Temporal Goods

7. Carl Jung, "Paracelsus," in *The Spirit in Man, Art, and Literature*, trans. R. F. C. Hull (Princeton, NJ: Princeton University Press, 1969), 450.

8. Edith Wharton, *The House of Mirth* (New York: Bantam, 1984), 131–32.

9. Erik H. Erikson, *Childhood and Society* (New York: Norton, 1963), 266–67.

10. Sheldon Vanauken, *A Severe Mercy* (San Francisco: Harper & Row, 1980), 36–37.

11. Ibid., 37, 48.

12. C. S. Lewis, *The Screwtape Letters* (New York: Macmillan, 1961), 56.

13. F. Scott Fitzgerald, "The Crack-Up," in *The Crack-Up*, ed. Edmund Wilson (New York: New Direction Books, 1945), 69, 72, 74.

14. St. Thomas Aquinas, *Summa Theologica*, II, II, Q. 118, a. 8.

15. Dante, *Convivio*, trans. William Walrond Jackson (Oxford, UK: Clarendon, 1909), 239–40.

16. Leo Tolstoy, "The King and the Shirt," in *Fables and Fairy Tales*, trans. Ann Dunnigan (New York: New American Library, 1962), 20.

17. Ibid., 21.

18. St. Thomas Aquinas, *Summa Theologica*, II, II, Q. 117, a. 2. reply.

19. Ibid., II, II, Q. 117, a. 2. reply; italics added.

20. Aristotle, *Ethics* 4.1.

21. Rainer Maria Rilke, *The Selected Poems of Rainer Maria Rilke*, trans. Stephen Mitchell (New York: Vintage, 1982), 263.

Joy in Natural Goods

22. John Cheever, "O Youth and Beauty!" in *The Stories of John Cheever* (New York: Ballantine, 1978), 250.

23. Ibid., 249.

24. Ibid., 254.

25. Ibid., 254–55.

26. Ibid., 256.

27. Ibid., 257.

28. Ibid., 258–59.

29. Edith Wharton, *The House of Mirth* (New York: Bantam, 1984), 286.

30. St. Thomas Aquinas, *Summa Theologica*, II, II, Q. 115, a. 2.

31. Cicero, "De Amicitia," trans. Cyrus R. Edmonds, in *Friendship: Marcus Tullius Cicero, Francis Bacon, Ralph Waldo Emerson*, Harvard College Library Series (Chicago: Albert & Scott, 1890), 58.

Joy in Sensory Goods

32. John Climacus, *The Ladder of Divine Ascent*, trans. Colin Luibheid and Norman Russell (New York: Paulist Press, 1982), 179.

33. St. Thomas Aquinas, *Summa Theologica*, II, II, Q. 141, a. 2.

Joy in Moral Goods

34. Frederick Faber, "On Taking Scandal," in *Spiritual Conferences* (Philadelphia: Peter Reilly, 1957), 251.

35. Charles Dickens, *A Christmas Carol and Other Christmas Stories* (New York: Signet Classics, 1984), 39.

36. For a good treatment of the Scholastic division of the passions, see Paul Wadell's book *The Primacy of Love: An Introduction to the Ethics of Thomas Aquinas* (Mahwah, NJ: Paulist Press, 1992), 96–97.

Joy in Spiritual Goods

37. J. R. R. Tolkien, *The Letters of J. R. R. Tolkien*, ed. Humphrey Carpenter (Boston: Houghton Mifflin, 1981), 339.

38. Thomas à Kempis, *The Imitation of Christ*, trans. Aloysius Croft and Harold Bolton (Mineola, NY: Dover, 2003), 22.

39. Thomas Hardy, "In Church," in *Thomas Hardy: The Complete Poems* (New York: Macmillan, 1976), 16.

40. St. Gregory the Great, *Pastoral Care*, trans. Henry Davis (Westminster, MD: Newman, 1950), 234.

41. T. S. Eliot, *Murder in the Cathedral* (New York: Harcourt, Brace & Jovanovich, 1963), 45.

42. John Henry Newman, "Personal Influence: The Means of Propagating the Truth," in *Oxford University Sermons* (London: Longmans, Green, 1892), 92, 95.

43. St. Augustine, *Teaching Christianity*, trans. Edmund Hill, O.P. (Hyde Park, NY: New City Press, 1996), 218.

Conclusion

44. Christoph Wolff, *Johann Sebastian Bach: The Learned Musician* (New York: Norton, 2000), 443.

INDEX

About Us

ICS Publications, based in Washington, D.C., is the publishing house of the Institute of Carmelite Studies (ICS) and a ministry of the Discalced Carmelite Friars of the Washington Province (U.S.A.) The Institute of Carmelite Studies promotes research and publication in the field of Carmelite spirituality, especially about Carmelite saints and related topics. Its members are friars of the Washington Province.

Discalced Carmelites are a worldwide Roman Catholic religious order comprised of friars, nuns, and laity—men and women who are heirs to the teaching and way of life of Teresa of Avila and John of the Cross, dedicated to contemplation and to ministry in the church and the world.

Information about their way of life is available through local diocesan vocation offices, or from the Discalced Carmelite Friars vocation directors at the following addresses:

Washington Province:
1525 Carmel Road, Hubertus, WI, 53033

California-Arizona Province:
P.O. Box 446, Redlands, CA 92373

Oklahoma Province:
5151 Marylake Drive, Little Rock, AR 72206

Visit our websites at:
www.icspublications.org and *www.ocdfriarsvocation.org*